Mary Wigman   „Tanz in der Stille"

Foto S. Enkelmann Berlin

Frontispiece *Dance in Stillness* from the dance cycle *Autumnal Dances*, 1937. Photograph by Siegfried Enkelman, courtesy of the Arkiv Darstellende Kunst, Akademie der Künste, Berlin

MARY WIGMAN

Routledge Performance Practitioners is a series of introductory guides to the key theater-makers of the last century. Each volume explains the background to and the work of one of the major influences on twentieth and twenty-first-century performance.

A dancer, teacher and choreographer, Mary Wigman was a leading innovator in Expressionist dance. Her radical explorations of movement and dance theory are credited with expanding the scope of dance as a theatrical art in her native Germany and beyond. This book combines for the first time:

- a full account of Wigman's life and work
- detailed discussion of her aesthetic theories, including the use of space as an "invisible partner" and the transcendent nature of performance
- a commentary on her key works, including *Hexentanz* and *The Seven Dances of Life*.
- an extensive collection of practical exercises designed to provide an understanding of Wigman's choreographic principles and her uniquely immersive approach to dance.

As a first step towards critical understanding, and as an initial exploration before going on to further primary research, **Routledge Performance Practitioners** are unbeatable value for today's student.

Mary Anne Santos Newhall is Assistant Professor of Dance at the University of New Mexico. She is also research director for the American Dance Legacy Institute at Brown University.

ROUTLEDGE PERFORMANCE PRACTITIONERS

Series editor: Franc Chamberlain, University College Cork

Routledge Performance Practitioners is an innovative series of introductory handbooks on key figures in twentieth-century performance practice. Each volume focuses on a theater-maker whose practical and theoretical work has in some way transformed the way we understand theater and performance. The books are carefully structured to enable the reader to gain a good grasp of the fundamental elements underpinning each practitioner's work. They will provide an inspiring springboard for future study, unpacking and explaining what can initially seem daunting.

The main sections of each book cover:

- personal biography
- explanation of key writings
- description of significant productions
- reproduction of practical exercises.

Volumes currently available in the series are:

Eugenio Barba by Jane Turner
Pina Bausch by Royd Climenhaga
Augusto Boal by Frances Babbage
Bertolt Brecht by Meg Mumford
Michael Chekhov by Franc Chamberlain
Jacques Copeau by Mark Evans
Etienne Decroux by Thomas Leabhart
Jerzy Grotowski by James Slowiak and Jairo Cuesta
Anna Halprin by Libby Worth and Helen Poyner
Rudolf Laban Karen K. Bradley
Robert Lepage by Aleksandar Dundjerovic
Ariane Mnouchkine by Judith G. Miller
Jacques Lecoq by Simon Murray
Joan Littlewood by Nadine Holdsworth
Vsevolod Meyerhold by Jonathan Pitches

Future volumes will include:

MARY WIGMAN

Mary Anne Santos Newhall

 Routledge
Taylor & Francis Group

LONDON AND NEW YORK

First published 2009
by Routledge
2 Park Square, Milton Park, Abingdon, Oxon OX14 4RN

Simultaneously published in the USA and Canada
by Routledge
270 Madison Avenue, New York, NY 10016

Routledge is an imprint of the Taylor & Francis Group, an informa business

Typeset in Perpetua and Akzidenz Grotesk by
Taylor & Francis Books
Printed and bound in Great Britain by
CPI Antony Rowe, Chippenham, Wiltshire

British Library Cataloguing in Publication Data
A catalogue record for this book is available from the British Library

Library of Congress Cataloging in Publication Data
  Newhall, Mary Anne Santos.
  Mary Wigman / Mary Anne Santos Newhall.
    p. cm.
  Includes bibliographical references and index.
  1. Wigman, Mary, 1886–1973. 2. Dancers – Germany – Biography.
3. Choreographers – Germany – Biography. 4. Modern dance – Social
aspects – Germany – History. 5. Modern dance – Political aspects –
Germany – History. 6. Modern dance – Philosophy. I. Title.
  GV1785.W5N49 2008
  792.802'8092 – dc22
[B]
                                                  2008016966

ISBN10: 0-415-37526-6 (hbk)
ISBN10: 0-415-37527-4 (pbk)
ISBN10: 0-203-09898-6 (ebk)

ISBN13: 978-0-415-37526-9 (hbk)
ISBN13: 978-0-415-37527-6 (pbk)
ISBN13: 978-0-203-09898-1 (ebk)

FOR MARY

CONTENTS

FIGURES

ACKNOWLEDGMENTS

Perhaps it is best to begin at the beginning. Work on this book started nearly fifteen years ago, and if anyone had predicted at that time that I would spend the ensuing years researching the life and work of Mary Wigman, I would have shaken my head in disbelief. And curiously, this journey was first inspired by an American modern dance pioneer. Eve Gentry was a quintessential American modern, born to a Jewish immigrant family and finding her way to the New York dance community in 1936 when she became a member of the original Hanya Holm company. What Eve gave to me, a dancer who came of age in the late 1970s, was nothing short of a revelation. The great tradition of the German modern dance was unknown to me before I met Eve and, like most of my contemporaries, I had lived with the myth that the modern dance was uniquely American. I had my own prejudices against things German as an American child of the post-Second World War era. That this small Jewish dancer could open my eyes to the monolithic German dance so immediately is a testimony to Eve's own power, the strength of her work and the complexities of cultural history. Eve died before I could ask her the many questions that have arisen as I traced her dance lineage back to Mary Wigman. But her papers have revealed much over the past decade and I thank Michele Larsson for making them available to me. It was always the dance that spoke to me, deepening my understanding even as I navigated the scholarly channels in this work.

As for the help that it takes to continue such a quest, I have many to thank. First, Judith Chazin-Bennahum for her ongoing support and deep reading of my draft manuscript. In so many ways, her graciousness and her authority in the field have served to ground my work. I have also had the support of my friends and colleagues at the University of New Mexico: Donna Jewell, my boss and comrade; Eva Encinias-Sandoval, an inspiration through the example of her own dedication to her field; and Jane Slaughter, historian and advisor extraordinaire, who has kept me on course as a historian, along with the professors in UNM's History Department: Melissa Bokovoy, Charlie Steen, Melvin Yazawa and Eliza Ferguson.

Most importantly, Jennifer Predock-Linnell and Jim Linnell have been much more than mentors; they are kindred spirits, encouraging curiosity and genuine creativity in performance and writing. Their friendship has been one of the greatest gifts in a project of vast riches. And, of course, I thank my students at the University. In technique and lecture classes, they have been willing and curious experimenters as I brought the strangest ideas to them. Dena Kinney, director of the Fine Arts Library, has been an ever-enthusiastic resource, and I have had much help from the library staff at UNM along with those at St. John's College in Santa Fe and the Mesa Vista Library in Los Alamos, who have allowed me to find productive places to undertake the sitting practice that is writing. The hardworking visionaries of the American Dance Legacy Institute at Brown University, Julie Strandberg, Carolyn Adams and Laura Bennett, all have contributed to this writing through their genuine understanding of what it means to be a dance practitioner and scholar, and I am always at home when I am with them.

Because of a research grant from UNM, I have many archives to thank, for the labors of the archivists make such research possible. I am especially grateful to Frank-Manuel Peter and Garnet Schuldt-Hiddemann at the Tanzarchiv in Köln and Inge Baxmann, Melanie Gruss and Gabriela Ruiz at the Tanzarchiv in Leipzig, where the hospitality of Barbara and Dieter Wellner made my extended stay possible. Many thanks especially to Stephan Dörschel at the Archiv Darstellende Kunst in Berlin who remains helpful in my continuing research. Norbert Busè and Christof Debler of Filmhouse in Berlin helped me to see Wigman's history firsthand in Hellerau, Dresden and Berlin. Most importantly, I thank Hedwig Müller, Mary Wigman's

German biographer, whose telling of Wigman's story and deep understanding of Wigman's humanity has graced this writing in more ways than I can express.

My deepest thanks go to Brigitta Herrmann, whose love for Mary Wigman as a teacher shines through our many hours of discussions and who was the source of so much embodied knowledge of Wigman's teaching practices. In part, this book is dedicated to Brigitta's unique personality and vision and the spirit of Mary Wigman that she keeps alive in her own work. And I also thank those American students of Mary Wigman who shared their memories: Bill Costanza, Sarah Manno and especially Sandy Broyard, who also generously shared her home on Martha's Vineyard. Herr and Frau Kurt Schwaen welcomed me into their home in Marlsdorf and carried me into Mary Wigman's life in Leipzig. Their sharing of letters and stories will ever remain etched in my memory.

I also thank Ellen Lefkowitz, who nimbly and lovingly guided my understanding of the psychological underpinnings of the subject and author of this work. My only sadness at the end of this project is that Claire McKibben is not here to see it born. I miss her razor-sharp wit and unquenchable belief in me and I always will.

I thank my editor, Franc Chamberlain of Routledge, whose very trusting way of working has actually made the editing process enjoyable.

And finally, I thank my family: Jesse, who has declared our home "dance central" and most of all my thanks and love to Jim, who has been a diligent copy editor, highly over-qualified research assistant and patient partner. Without his loving help and support, none of this would have been possible.

MARY WIGMAN: A LIFE IN DANCE

"Strong and convincing art has never arisen from theories."

Mary Wigman

PROLOGUE: WHY MARY WIGMAN?

Mary Wigman was the best-known ambassador of German dance during the interwar period, as her touring took her across Europe and to the United States. Promotional literature for those tours sought to educate the public about this new art phenomenon, and critics responded with enthusiasm and keen attention, if not always with praise. When US critic John Martin published 'The Dance' in 1946 he placed Wigman in the highest constellation of dance artists, in part for her artistic creations and especially for how she widened the range and advanced the underlying theories of the art. Following the Second World War, however, Wigman received only fleeting attention in the English-language historiography of modern dance. In fact, the whole of early German *Ausdruckstanz*, or dance of expression, was barely discussed in postwar writing on dance modernism, which centered on the American modern dance pioneers and US dance developments. One later exception was the work of Pina Bausch, whose career began in Germany, continued in the United States and then returned to Germany in the form of *Tanztheatre*.

Don McDonagh's *The Rise and Fall and Rise of Modern Dance* (1970) mentions Wigman only in passing. McDonagh's contention was that modern dance "had been created out of the American experience in the same manner in which jazz had been created" (McDonagh 1970: 1). Anti-German sentiment, which ran high during and after the war, offers one explanation of why scholars failed to acknowledge the enormous impact of early modern German dance, and Wigman's work in particular. In *Time and the Dancing Image*, Deborah Jowitt wrote, "quite a few early reviews presuppose some influence from Germany on the major American modernists, if only as a catalyst. ... it remains a moot point how directly and to what extent [German dancers] may have [influenced the Americans]" (Jowitt 1988: 167–8). Bronner and Kellner claimed, "The role of dance, both as a motif and as a topic of discussion, has not been dealt with in any systematic way in German literary history" (Bronner and Kellner 1983: 351). Fortunately, Walter Sorell assembled and translated some of Wigman's writings in the 1960s and 1970s and Horst Koegler wrote comprehensively about the period in English and in German. But no one produced an in-depth Wigman biography until 1986, when Hedwig Müller came forward as Wigman's primary biographer. The publication of *Mary Wigman: Leben und Werk der grossen Tanzerin* (Mary Wigman: Life and Work of the Great Dancer) appears definitive and is supported by a great deal of the dancer's own writings. Müller's assiduous research and sensitive reading of Wigman's papers allow insight into her world. Unfortunately, Müller's book has not been translated into English, but such a translation would be a major contribution to the understanding of Wigman's story in the English language.

In 1993, the publication of Susan Manning's *Ecstasy and the Demon: Feminism and Nationalism in the Dances of Mary Wigman* returned Wigman to the scholarly spotlight. Manning's writing drew on a wide range of sources, including Müller's biography. Through analysis of choreographed works, Manning set out to reveal Wigman with a new emphasis. Manning's book sheds much light on Wigman's work. In addition, she sought to question Wigman's accommodations with the National Socialist government. She presents Wigman possibly as a proto-fascist and, if not a willing collaborator, then a less-than-naive participant within the Nazi regime. In *Hitler's Dancers*, Lillian Karina and Marion Kant build on Manning's analysis, citing carefully selected archival evidence to propose reconsidering Wigman, and others, as

Nazi sympathizers and thus culpable, particularly in light of her engagement with the *Reichskulturkammer* from 1933 until 1937 under Propaganda Minister Joseph Goebbels.

Acclaimed and accused, Mary Wigman emerges as a genuinely original and multi-faceted human being, one who devoted her life to dance in an era remarkable in its artistic innovation as well as its staggering tragedy. There are no simple answers or clear-cut conclusions in Wigman's story. From the earliest German articles and critiques dedicated to her oeuvre, through the more recent contributions of Karl Toepfer, Michael Huxley, Norbert Servos, Gabriele Fritsch-Vivé, Diane Howe, Valerie Preston-Dunlop and Isa Partsch-Bergshon, many have written about this period in German dance history and Mary Wigman's place in that history.

In a 2005 review, Marion Kant poses a paradoxical question, "Which modern dancer would not like to trace her training and artistic roots back to Wigman, if only through a summer course?" (Kant 2005: 417). Perhaps, given the ongoing fascination and controversy swirling around Mary Wigman's life and work, another question should be posed, "Why does Mary Wigman still matter?" Are there elements of her work that remain relevant or revelatory for contemporary artists?

Seemingly forgotten by postmodern dancers of the twenty-first century, Wigman's life and work are drawing renewed interest among dance and theater artists in Germany and beyond. Even while modernism by its very nature privileges the new over the past, it seems compelling to consider Wigman's life and work once again. Perhaps enough time has passed since the Second World War to allow objective reflection on the genius and the humanness of Mary Wigman both as an inspiration and as a cautionary tale for our time. Perhaps this reflects an impulse toward a new kind of expressionism for the twenty-first century. And perhaps this is an indication of some commonalities between the *Zeitgeist* of this new millennium and that of the last century. The human body in dance remains a most immediate barometer of the state of the individual body within the world body. And Mary Wigman's life and work offer an exceptional reflection of her world.

The purpose of this book is a simple one. It is meant to serve as a general introduction to Wigman and is organized in four sections. The first section tells the story of her life and the times in which she lived, with highlights of the outstanding moments of her long career. The second section analyzes Wigman's writings with an eye to understanding how her art reveals her philosophy, placing it within related artistic and philosophical movements. The third section focuses on some of her major choreographic works. The final section outlines a series of practical exercises, with particular attention to Wigman's pedagogy. These exercises are intended to give the experimenter a visceral experience of the performance and training elements that appear most crucial to understanding Mary Wigman's perspective. They exercises are in no way meant to recreate Wigman's teaching practice, but are simply intended to provide one contemporary way of experiencing the fundamental elements identified by Wigman as she formulated her deep exploration into the stuff that dance is made of. Certainly, there is much more to analyze, debate and discover about her life and work and this text is written in the hope of encouraging such continued research and creative endeavors.

INTRODUCTION

Mary Wigman was born into a middle-class West Prussian family in 1886 and made Germany her home until her death in Berlin in 1973. Her life serves as a prism for viewing the complexity and immense difficulty of her era. She took part in the primary avant-garde art movements of the twentieth century and was eventually a principal founder and transmitter of the *Ausdruckstanz* or expressive dance movement. Wigman's remarkable career spanned the era of the Wilhelmine Empire, the Weimar Republic, the Third Reich and the years of a divided Germany following the Second World War. Not only was she present for the most cataclysmic political changes of her age, but also, as an artistic innovator, she stands as a seminal figure in the conception of what has come to be known as the modern dance.

Ausdruckstanz (expressive dance)

Absoluter tanz (absolute dance) – defined by Wigman as dancing pure and simple, without lights, dance or costume to decorate an idea or conceal its lack. (The origin of the term is attributed to different sources. Apparently it was introduced by Laban or first used by Wigman in a Dada performance art piece with Sophie Tauber. Historically, Absolute was a Hegelian term first used by Fichte.)

Freier tanz (free dance)

Neuer künstlerischer tanz (new artistic dance)

All these terms were renamed German Dance by the Cultural Ministry under the Third Reich.

Her *Ausdruckstanz* was fundamental to the development of dance and theater in Germany and beyond. Her aesthetic ideas were disseminated throughout Europe and traveled to the United States through her touring from 1929–32 and continued with the establishment of the Mary Wigman School in New York City in 1931. The myriad, widespread uses of dance improvisation as a tool for movement development, as a vehicle for performance and even as a method for physical and psychological therapy all have their roots deep in the work of Mary Wigman.

Wigman's work also can be viewed as an assimilation of the major artistic innovations of her time: Romanticism, Symbolism, Primitivism, Expressionism and Dada art, all gathered under the banner of Modernism. Wigman's life can act as a personal guide to these movements and their primary characters. As a child of the rising bourgeoisie of late nineteenth-century Germany, she used her body as a place of resistance against the expectations of her own family and the larger society. Her early years of training were spent with two great twentieth-century systematizers of movement: Emile Jaques-Dalcroze at the garden city of Hellerau and Rudolf von Laban at the utopian community of Monte Verità in Ascona, Switzerland. She was a muse for the Expressionist painters Emil Nolde, Ernst Kirchner, Oskar Schlemmer and others. And she performed alongside the most radical Dada artists at the Café Voltaire. Her time as a working artist during the rise and fall of the Third Reich offers a lens through which to view those terrible years, and what came after. From her own writing, it is possible to deduce what she might most wish to be remembered for. Throughout her life her focus was on one thing: the dance. In the end, it is her passion for dance and her artistic innovations that endure and also offer tools to reinvigorate contemporary dance and theater. Her innovations are many and include:

- her unique concept of space as an invisible and truly sensual partner in the dance
- her rejection of ballet technique with a fervor equal to that of her fellow dance pioneer Isadora Duncan
- her radical ideas about the relationship between music and the dance
- her use of theatrical elements – notably text – to create a *Gesamtkunstwerk*
- her development of von Laban's ideas for solo works, mass movement and group composition
- her fundamental belief in and demand for a modern emphasis on the transcendent nature and spiritual purpose of dance.

Gesamtkunstwerk – literally "total art work" incorporating technical theatrical elements, text, song, music and dance as integral elements of a total performance. The most prominent practitioner was Richard Wagner; however, Emile Jaques-Dalcroze with Adolf Appia and Laban and Wigman aspired to integrate all these elements into a total work.

Thus Wigman holds many titles in the world of dance and theater. She stands as a trailblazer, a stunning soloist and astute choreographer, a pedagogue and theoretician, an inspiration for many artists who followed, a conflicted figure caught in the political drama of her time, an intellectual, a mystic and the most pragmatic of arts administrators. The complexity of Wigman's persona cannot be overstated, but the real heart of this artist appears in her work as a consummate performer. This, for Wigman, was the moment of transcendence:

But above the consummation of creation and ambition to succeed in a profession, there emerges something quite colossal and wonderful – a climax of achievement, which comes to you as a glorious gift from the gods. These are the rare moments in which, completely carried beyond yourself and removed from reality, you are the vessel of an idea. In these rare moments you carry the blazing torch which emits the spark jumping from the "I" to the "we," from dancer to spectator. This is the moment of divine consummation, when the fire dances between the two poles, when the personal experience of the creator is communicated to those who watch.

(Wigman 1973: 170)

CHILDHOOD

Mary Wigman was born **Karoline Sofie Marie Wiegmann** on 13 November 1886 in Hanover, Germany. Without a doubt, Mary Wigman was a true child of her age who turned her own body into a canvas for the palette of that *Zeitgeist*. She was born a Wilhelmine woman whose parents, Amelie and Heinrich Wiegmann, reaped significant benefits from the expansion that was transforming the German economy. With the unification of Germany in 1871 and the sharp rise of industrialization, a burgeoning middle class was riding a wave of new wealth that also carried the Wiegmann family toward the twentieth century. Heinrich and his brothers, August and Dietrich, built a successful family business selling and repairing bicycles and sewing machines, products that represented the incursion of the machine age into the everyday lives of middle-class Germans. Many families had gone from working class to middle class in a single generation. Mary was the first-born. Her brother Heinrich came along four years later and her younger sister Elisabeth was born in 1894. When Mary was nine years old her father died. Three years later her mother married Dietrich Wiegmann and her uncle became her stepfather. Thus her early life was circumscribed by home and the family business.

Karoline Sofie Marie Wiegmann – birth name of Mary Wigman.

Bright and accomplished at school, Wigman wanted to continue on to *Gymnasium*. Instead, her family sent her brother to secondary school and Mary received lessons in language and music, social dancing and comportment. In 1901, at the age of fourteen, she went to a girls' school at Folkestone on England's south coast for a few months and the following year she traveled to Lausanne, Switzerland. She learned English and French, but the goal of this education was solely to make her an attractive and marriageable *Hausfrau*, one able to contribute to the well-being and upward social mobility of her family. And she would have none of it. She had always identified herself as an adventurous spirit. While at school in England there were stories about a secret passage hidden within the town church. In *The Mary Wigman Book*, she recalls with obvious relish and some pride that she "bought a little hammer and went to tap the walls and listen for a hollow echo" (Wigman 1973: 28). Just as she listened for the echoes in the church walls, Mary Wigman was compelled to turn her attention toward her own inner landscape. Her greatest drive was to express what she described as the stirrings within her.

Gymnasium – secondary school in the German system.

Searching to find an outlet through which to express these inner stirrings, Wigman had thought that she might become a singer. Her singing teacher said, "You have a good voice and you have a way of expression I have never seen before. You could make a career." But her family said no (Wigman 1973: 186). Keeping with their expectations, she was twice formally engaged to marry, only to have both engagements fail. After the second ended she wrote,

> I cried, I begged, and asked my creator to bring me clarity. I didn't know what I should do, I had to break away, I didn't want to continue any longer, I could not. The entire bourgeois life collapsed on to me, you might say.
>
> (Wigman in Manning 1993: 50)

Like many youth of her time, Wigman was caught between an old order of prescribed roles and the new world of possibilities that were an outgrowth of economic success. She had traveled and experienced a world far beyond what was available to most women of her mother's generation, yet she was expected to put all of her ambition to the service of her family. She saw hypocrisy in what she considered the superficial bourgeois respectability of her parents' generation and she and many members of her own age group would rebel in a fashion not unlike that seen again in the United States of America and Western Europe in the 1960s and 1970s.

Coming of age in the first decade of the twentieth century, Wigman appeared to have few options available to her. Certainly the life of an artist seemed far from every expectation put upon her by family and society in general. Yet she was swept along by the tide of modern attitudes toward art and life. In 1900 Ezra Pound had challenged the modern artist to "Make it New!" Wigman and her contemporaries responded

Figure 1 Marie Wiegmann at 20 in Hanover, 1906. Photograph by Alex Möhlen, courtesy of the Deutsche Tanzarchiv Köln

with a radical change in the very way they fashioned their lives. A life-affirming *Körperkultur* or physical culture arose on both sides of the Atlantic, encouraging fitness and a new sort of bodily expression of emotion. And just as the emancipation of women was being pioneered, **Isadora Duncan**'s introduction of "uncorseted" dance opened new avenues for dancers to follow in her wake. It is important to remember that Mary Wigman came to dance in her late twenties. A ballet career was never a possibility. Nor did she desire one. She and her cohorts indeed had to make the dance art new in order to express the experiences and conflicts of their age.

Isadora Duncan (1877–1927) – great innovator of the free dance. She traveled the Western world sowing the seeds of the barefoot aesthetic dance movement. In 1904 she briefly established a school in Germany, and in 1921 one in Moscow. She introduced a concert dance form that was non-narrative, feminist, but still tightly bound to the music, so much so that she drew scorn from music critics at the time. She remains the progenitor of dance modernism.

THE BEGINNING OF A LIFE IN DANCE

Following the end of her first engagement in 1905, Mary Wigman was sent to visit her aunt in Amsterdam. There she saw the pupils of **Emile Jaques-Dalcroze** in a demonstration of *Eurhythmie*, his system designed to wed music and movement through practical experience. His students performed Carl Maria von Weber's *Invitation to the Waltz* and for Wigman it was a revelation of a new way of approaching musical expression through bodily interpretation. Over the next five years, Wigman would return to the dance again and again in her search for a life's path.

Emile Jaques-Dalcroze (1865–1950) – established a dance institute, *Der Bildungsanstalt für Musik und Rhythmus* (Educational Institute for Music and Rhythm), in Hellerau in 1910. Introduced an analytical approach to dance education through a systematic study of the fundamentals of music embodied using codified movement. Collaborated with innovating stage designer **Adolph Appia (1862–1928)**, who created a new way of designing the stage using "rhythmic spaces" formed by tiered platforms and stairs that added architectural dimension to the space. Appia's ideas traveled to the United States through the work of Arch Lauterer, stage designer for the Bennington choreographers, Graham, Humphrey and Holm.

Eurhythmie or Eurhythmics – Emile Jaques-Dalcroze's system of linking sound to physical action designed to help in the training of musicians and to facilitate their motor memory. Dalcroze felt that rhythm unites the physical body with the spiritual, thus bringing the whole being into harmony. It is one example of the fin de siècle propensity to systematize, or to organize or arrange by a system that could be codified. Exemplars include Jaques-Dalcroze, Rudolf von Laban and **Arnold Schoenberg**. Eurythmy is the name of a separate system developed by anthroposophist Rudolf Steiner.

By 1908 Mary Wigman was twenty-two years old, still living in the family home and plunging toward her family's greatest fear: that she would become an overeducated "Old Maid." She had also ended another engagement and was deeply unhappy. In her memoirs, she describes closing herself in a room and crying in desperation at her situation. And she found that when she cried she made movements with her hands as she paced. During this period of despair, Wigman saw a performance by the three **Wiesenthal** sisters, Elsa, Berta and Grete. The Wiesenthals were dancing celebrities and Grete, in particular, became well known for her interpretation of the Viennese waltz, representing the elegance, grace and style of fin de siècle Vienna. Seeing Grete Wiesenthal's performance of The Beautiful Blue Danube at the opera house in Hanover, Wigman felt a new world opening before her. In her memoirs, Wigman appears to have been especially taken by the beauty of Wiesenthal's hands in the dance, as well the range of emotions that the hands could convey. Hedwig Müller describes Wigman as being intoxicated by the movement: "hands that can laugh happily and also express struggle, sadness and the gentleness of the dance" (Müller

1986a: 19). Perhaps in this moment Wigman recognized the cry of her own hands dancing the despair of her heart while she was locked away in the guest room of her family home. Here was the outlet for expression for which she had been searching. She approached the Wiesenthals, hoping to study with them. She was told that at twenty-two she was too old to begin to dance. In her memoirs she reminisced that one teacher advised, "My dear girl, go home and be a *Hausfrau* — you'll be happier ... You'll never be a dancer" (Wigman 1973: 27). Yet she persisted. She again saw a demonstration of *Eurhythmie* by Dalcroze's students and the way became clear to her. She said, "I want to do the same" (Wigman 1973: 187). Overcoming the resistance of her family and the "whole bourgeois world," she began her life in dance at the age of twenty-seven under the tutelage of Emile Jaques-Dalcroze.

Grete Wiesenthal (1885–1972) – the most famous of the Wiesenthal Sisters performing group, Grete was considered the most important dancer in Vienna during the first two decades of the twentieth century and was said to embody the spirit of the waltz for which that city was famous.

DALCROZE AND THE GARDEN CITY OF HELLERAU

The beginning of the twentieth century saw many systematizers like Jaques-Dalcroze, theorists who turned to art in order to create an organized system in response to the chaos and uncertainty of the age. While **Arnold Schoenberg** later would reshape Western music with the twelve-tone scale, cubists Picasso and Braque would dissect and reassemble the familiar human form, and James Joyce would restructure the written word, Jaques-Dalcroze codified a method of applying gesture and movement to corresponding musical elements. Jaques-Dalcroze was considered a leader in art education by 1910, the year he established his school in the planned **Garden City of Hellerau** situated five miles outside of Dresden. Mary Wigman literally ran away from home to become a member of that community.

> **Garden City movement** – construction of the Garden City of Hellerau was begun in 1908 by the German Garden City Association, founded six years earlier, in cooperation with the *Deutschen Werkstätten* (German Workshops). A consistent feature of the German *Lebensreform* or living reform movement in the early 1900s was the call for cooperatively owned "garden cities." The living reformers, mostly literati and leftist Social Democratic activists, initially envisioned the garden cities as a response to the housing crisis in Wilhelmine-era urban centers.

> **Hellerau** – In 1908, a parcel of urban land in Germany cost up to seven times more than a comparable plot in England. By setting the new town of German industrialist Karl Schmitt (1873–1948) upon the rolling hills outside Dresden, planners could design an entire community from the ground up. The design emphasized low-density building as well as collective housing layouts. The plans conveyed a nostalgia for rural villages of the nineteenth century, as well as a social message that true communities required a firm sense of place, a harmony of interests, and a marriage of livelihood and cultural pursuits. The education of the children of the community was considered equally important as humane working conditions for their parents. Hellerau was conceived as a sort of planning *Gesamtkunstwerk* that integrated many aspects of public and private life.

Many artists were drawn to Hellerau. Due to its proximity to Dresden, members of the **Expressionist** painters group *Die Brücke* (The Bridge) became part of the Hellerau circle. One member of this group, **Emil Nolde**, would become a close personal friend of Wigman. Most of Wigman's biographers mention Nolde as the person who introduced her to dance theoretician **Rudolf von Laban** in 1913; however, the relationship between Nolde's painting and Wigman's choreography warrants greater consideration. In Wigman's autobiography, she describes their artistic relationship:

> My acquaintanceship – I had better say my friendship – with the painter Emil Nolde dated far back … Nolde, whenever possible, came to my dance concerts. The managers knew about him and were aware of what was expected

from them. They reserved three seats: one for him, one for his tubes and pots of paints, and one for his wife, who stood guard lest he should be disturbed. I don't know what happened to those on-the-scene sketches. The few he gave me were destroyed when Dresden was bombed.

(Wigman 1973: 55)

Expressionism – Expressionism refers to particular German visual art movements of the pre-First World War period. By definition, Expressionism looks within to reveal a world of emotional and psychological states. With Van Gogh, the Fauves, Gauguin and Edvard Munch as points of departure, these painters distorted figures, applied strong colors and exaggerated forms. The Expressionists shared the conviction that art could express an intrinsic human truth and thus restore meaning to people's lives. In its narrowest sense, Expressionism refers to particular German visual art movements of the pre-First World War period. *Die Brücke* and **Der Blaue Reiter** groups housed the best-known proponents of the movement. Their development closely parallels Wigman's own, both in philosophical and in aesthetic values.

Die Brücke – (The Bridge) *Die Brücke* rejected the classical inheritance and turned to nature and the primal to renew German art. Most of its members moved to Berlin between 1910 and 1914. Members included Erich Heckel, Ernst Ludwig Kirchner, Max Pechstein, Karl Schmidt-Rotluff and briefly Emile Nolde, the group's eldest member.

Der Blaue Reiter – (The Blue Rider) *Der Blaue Reiter* group was more overtly mystical and claimed to reveal the spiritual truth hidden within the physical world. These painters, among them Franz Marc and Alexei von Jawlensky, were strongly influenced by the Russian painter Wassily Kandinsky and used a subtler range of colors than did *Die Brücke* artists.

Emile Nolde (1867–1956) – German Expressionist painter, member of *Die Brücke* and friend of Mary Wigman. His interest in primitive art prompted him to participate in an expedition from 1913–14 to New Guinea via Russia and China. He was declared a degenerate artist by the Nazis in 1937 although he had been a member of the National Socialist Party.

Rudolf von Laban (1879–1958) – born in Bratislava, Austro-Hungary and enrolled in the Military Academy at Vienna Neustadt in 1899 by his father, the military governor of Herzegovina and Bosnia. Before graduation, he left the Academy to pursue the life of an artist. He moved to Munich, then Paris, then Schwabing, stayed in a sanatorium outside Dresden and wound up at Monte Verità in 1912. Laban sought to create a systematic analysis of dance movement based on fundamentals of weight or force, time and space unique to the movement art. He also developed a system of dance notation.

Indeed, *Die Brücke* painters were opposed to the usual practice of drawing static models. They became most interested in capturing physical movement, in the same way that **August Rodin** had captured movement in his sculpture. The loss of Nolde's sketches of Wigman is regrettable. However, a record of their early relationship does remain in his extant paintings, such as *Dance Around the Golden Calf*, one of many Nolde painted on Biblical subjects. The shapes of the dancers in *The Dance Round the Golden Calf* bear a strong resemblance to Wigman in a photograph of her earliest, 1914 version of the *Hexentanz*. There are obvious similarities in the angles of knees, ankles and elbows and the way that the feet are lifted off the ground while the skirts swirl, in both pictures. The photograph of Wigman and Nolde's painting both capture a sense of wild, abandoned movement, a hallmark of both Expressionist-era painting and dance.

August Rodin (1840–1917) – French sculptor who influenced the art form by the extremely lifelike character of his work, its expressive, light-catching surfaces, its concern with movement and passionate emotion and his treatment of the human body in works such as *The Kiss*, *The Thinker*, *Eternal Springtime* and *The Burghers of Calais*.

Figure 2 Emil Nolde, *Dance Around the Golden Calf*, 1910. Courtesy of the Staatsgalerie moderner Kunst, Munich

Like the Expressionist painters, Wigman and the practitioners of *Ausdruckstanz* were fully conscious of the visible world, but chose to look within and explore and present the mind, spirit and imagination. These artists were aware that humanity inhabits a number of complex, overlapping worlds and that these worlds, which are not seen by the eye, must be explored through the moving body. Their goal was the revealing of a new world of emotion and the mysterious motivations underlying human behavior. And they welcomed Sigmund Freud's identification of the subconscious. Just as Expressionist literature intends to startle the reader with subjective revelations of neurotic, often psychotic, states and just as the clashing dissonances of Expressionist music are intended to arouse rather than soothe the listener, *Ausdruckstanz* sought to produce a finished product that unsettled the viewer while finding a performance mode that took the dancer and her audience to the realm of transcendence and ritual. For Wigman and her cohorts, this flight into archaic rituals seemed at once regressive, progressive and an

Figure 3 Mary Wigman in the first version of *Hexentanz*, 1914. Photo reproduced by Rudolf von Delius, Dresden 1925, courtesy of the Tanzarchiv Leipzig

act of rebellion against their middle-class beginnings. They were joined in this rebellion by other dancers, artists and composers from beyond the borders of Germany.

By a calculated move of the *Ballets Russes* to Paris in 1909, **Serge Diaghilev** had been freed from the constrictions of the Imperial Ballet, whose repertory reflected the hierarchical social order of the empire, with soloists, demi-soloists and the chorus mirroring the monarchy, the aristocracy and the peasant class. Drawing together a stable of virtuosos, Diaghilev built a company that relied on the market economy instead of royal funding and began to produce ballets that shocked the Parisian art world. In 1913, Diaghilev, **Vaslav Nijinsky**, **Igor Stravinsky** and set designer **Nicholas Roerich** traveled from Paris to Germany while working on a new ballet, *Le Sacre du Printemps*, seeking to make a new myth of Russia by reaching back toward an idealized and imaginary, mythological past. Diaghilev took all of these artists to Hellerau to observe Jaques-Dalcroze's methods and incorporate them into the *Sacre*. Evidence of this influence is obvious, particularly in the second, *Sacrifice* section, where the driving rhythms and pathways in space appear to derive directly from Dalcroze's eurhythmic exercises. Over the span of the twentieth century and into the twenty-first, many dance companies would repeat the theme of the *Sacre*: of primal roots and individual sacrifice for the good of the group. It may well be the unifying myth of the modern age and it certainly has relevance to Mary Wigman's life. More than forty years later, Mary Wigman would set her own *Sacre du Printemps* at the Berlin Opera in 1957, her seventy-first year.

Serge Diaghilev (1872–1929) – impresario and director of the original *Ballets Russes*.

Vaslav Nijinsky (1889–1950) – virtuosic dancer, choreographer of *Afternoon of a Faun* and *Rite of Spring* for Diaghilev's *Ballets Russes*.

Igor Stravinsky (1882–1971) – influential modern composer. He composed *The Firebird, Petrouchka,* and *The Rite of Spring* for the *Ballets Russes*.

> **Nicholas Roerich (1874–1947)** – Russian painter, mystic and scenic designer for *Rite of Spring*.

But Wigman was still only a student at the time of Diaghilev's visit. She was becoming certified to teach the Dalcroze method, but already was growing disillusioned with its pedantic restrictiveness, particularly the way it limited dance in what she perceived as a slavish and subordinate relationship to music. Working alone in her room, Wigman had composed a dance work entitled *Lento* that was done in silence and reveled in the rhythm generated by the moving body itself. She showed the composition to Emil Nolde. He told her that there was another dancer who worked as she did and that she should seek him out. After taking part in Jaques-Dalcroze's preliminary production of C.W. Gluck's *Orpheus and Eurydice*, Wigman journeyed south from Hellerau to another community with a vision even more radically rebellious and emphatically utopian. It was here that Mary Wigman would commit herself to the path of dancer and choreographer.

RETURN TO RITUAL ON THE MOUNTAIN OF TRUTH

In 1913, Nolde encouraged Wigman to travel to Ascona, Switzerland, to enroll in Rudolf von Laban's *Schule der Bewegungskunst*, his summer school for the movement arts. Nolde had recognized that Laban's ideas about the possibilities of dance expression reflected Wigman's own. Laban's school flourished in the Alpine community of Monte Verità near Lago Maggiore. Founded as an experiment in the *Lebensreform* or life reform movement, those who sought to create a culture of artistic freedom at Monte Verità also espoused sexual freedom and feminism and rejected conservative ideas of respectability and hierarchical social order.

Martin Green claims that the avant-garde really began in 1900 with the establishment of the Monte Verità community, with the psychiatrist **Otto Gross** and pacifist **Gusto Gräser** among the founding figures. Many of those who formed the counterculture of the period between the turn of the century and the end of the First World War came through this commune. The founders of Monte Verità included anarchists, communists, alienists, vegetarians, theosophists and anthroposophists

influenced by Rudolf Steiner. At Monte Verità, independent artists such
as Paul Klee and Ernst Kirchner, and writers ranging from Dadaist
Hugo Ball to Herman Hesse, James Joyce, Rainer Maria Rilke and
D.H. Lawrence crossed paths. For the artists of Monte Verità, the act
of dancing came to represent an idealized return to the essential and
"natural" dimensions of human creative expression. For Mary Wigman
it was another revelation. After three weeks of Laban's summer course,
the morning post brought her notice of a job teaching the Dalcroze
method for which she had recently received her diploma. The job would
begin on 1 October. When she told Laban, instead of congratulating
her, he replied that it was a shame, that she was a dancer and belon-
ged on the stage. His reply was really an opening to her heart's desire.
She chose to stay (Müller 1986a: 43).

Otto Gross and Gusto Gräser – founding figures at Monte Verità.

Laban was beginning to work on concepts that would eventually
become his well-known theories of Space Harmony, movement analysis
and *Kinetographie Laban*, his popular form of dance notation. But
in the early years at Monte Verità these ideas were still in their nascent stages. While Laban, with Wigman's assistance, was beginning to
trace dance concepts that would eventually become pedagogical, the
primary choreographic influences on these dancers were grounded in
dance that was chthonic – rooted in nature and ritual. Wigman recalls
that the dancers "would camp down in a dell at the foot of a steep
rock which I climbed to improvise a wild witch dance" (Wigman
1973: 47). Indeed in 1914, Mary Wigman made her first version of
the *Hexentanz* and when Laban gave his approval she recounted jumping around the studio until she sprained her ankle, leaving her unable
to dance for a fortnight. Such was the effect of Laban's opinion at that
point in her career.

Kinetographie Laban **or Labanotation** – system of recording
dance movement through written symbols developed by Rudolf Laban
that remains the most widely used system of dance notation.

Figure 4 Marie Wiegmann becomes Mary Wigman at Monte Verità, summer 1914.
Photographer unknown, courtesy the Tanzarchiv Berlin

Combining ideas of *Festival* and *Körperkultur*, the dancers at Monte
Verità used dance to bring ceremony and significance to the very
shape of the day. Hedwig Müller and Norbert Servos write that such
flights into fantasy during the depths of trench warfare appear unsettling in hindsight (Müller and Servos 1982: 15–23). Indeed, the playful
naiveté exercised by Laban and company stood in stark contrast with
global realities. Monte Verità was a world unto itself until the larger
world overtook it. The summer of 1914 brought changes that ruptured
even the utopian dream at Monte Verità. On 1 August, Germany declared
war on Russia, on 3 August, Germany declared war on France and
crossed into Belgium, and the following day Great Britain declared
war on the German nation. The beginning of the First World War found
the community at Ascona emptying and Mary Wigman and Rudolf
von Laban were left to work together. Wigman served as a willing model
for Laban's ideas, particularly his development of the **swing scales**.
And the work was grueling for her. In contrast to her dramatic

nature, she had to analyze movement without the emphasis on emotion. However, she came to value Laban's more rational process in her own choreographic crafting.

> **Swing scale** – Laban's earliest studies of a codified method of warming the body while exploring dance fundamentals of space, time and effort.

In February of 1914 Mary Wigman had her first public performance in Munich. Ymelda Juliewna Mentelberg, a student of Laban, planned an evening of solo works demonstrating Laban's choreography and she asked Wigman to perform two of her own dances: *Lento* and the *Hexentanz*. It was a humble beginning; the stage was actually a creaky parquet platform in the beautiful old auditorium of the Munich museum. It was in this maiden performance that she first encountered the terrible, trembling stage fright that was to plague her thirty years on stage. But the miracle that would also occur time and again first came to her on that winter night. With the opening dancing gesture, all insecurity fell from her, "as if a magic word had been spoken. Only to have the chance to dance, to be able to dance was bliss" (Wigman 1973: 50). She made the decision to remain with Laban until she had acquired enough technical training to proceed on her own. She stayed with him for four more years.

DANCING DADA

Between summer and winter during the war years, Laban and his students moved between Ascona, Munich and Zurich. Once war had broken out, the neutral territory of Switzerland grew even more appealing and winter found Laban and his stable of acolytes entrenched in the Zurich cafes. Laban and his dancers were not the only ones of the Monte Verità group to relocate. Writer Hugo Ball was a catalyst whose magnetic presence united all the elements that eventually produced **Dada**. In 1916, Ball founded the Cabaret Voltaire, which came to be the center of the early Dada movement. Hans Richter, another key figure in the developing Dada, claimed that Dada was born in the confluence of poetry, theater, puppetry and dance.

> **Dada** – Dada emerged during the First World War. Shock was a key tactic for Dadaists, who hoped to shake society out of the nationalism and materialism that they felt had led to the carnage of the war. The first Dada manifesto of 1918 claimed that Dadaism was "a new reality" and accused the Expressionists "of sentimental resistance to the times."

> Our celestial headquarters was Laban's ballet school. There we met young dancers of our generation [including] Mary Wigman ... Only at certain fixed times were we allowed into this nunnery, with which we had emotional ties ... These highly personal contacts – and Laban's revolutionary contribution to choreography – finally involved the whole Laban school in the Dada movement ... dancers wearing [Marcel] Janco's abstract masks fluttered like butterflies of Ensor.
>
> (Richter 1965: 69–70)

Laban was clearly a man of great personal charisma and particular appeal to the young women who gathered around him as students. Regarding Laban's charm and the appeal of his "nunnery," Dadaist Richard Huelsenbeck reminisced:

> [Laban] would gather the most beautiful girls for his group. I really can't say whether I was drawn more to the beauty of the girls or the newness of the dancing. But since I've never particularly cared for, or understood much about the dance, I tend to think that I was drawn more to the beauty of the girls.
>
> (Huelsenbeck 1969: 11)

While the Dada impulse was intentionally full of paradox, it can be seen at its most basic as an attack that used exuberant creativity against a dysfunctional and decaying culture. In the Dada circle, the absurd was celebrated just as the raging of the Great War made an apparent absurdity of civilized existence. Certainly Wigman was drawn to the new and experimental nature of the Dada events. She was happy to claim a role in the inception of Dada.

> By the way do you know that your friend M. W. had an active share in the genesis of Dadaism? What divine feasts we have had in my Zürcher apartment! My friend Sophie Tauber – who later married [Dada artist] Hans Arp – and I

sewed ourselves so tightly into our extravagant costumes one day that, for the whole night we could not get out of them. And all the people of the Cafe Voltaire were my daily guests ...

(Wigman 1973: 141)

Wigman claimed that she adopted the term Absolute Dance at such a performance with Sophie Tauber. One credo for the Zurich Dadaists was "absolute poetry, absolute art, absolute dance" and Wigman was more than willing to take on that title for her own dance art. Indeed, the Expressionist goal of manifesting "truth" through art implies an acknowledgement of an absolute. In retrospect it seems that the Dada impulse was a transient inclination for Wigman. In truth the Dada manifestos claimed a turning away from the very Expressionist nature that her *Ausdruckstanz* embodied. For the Great Berlin Dada evening in April 1918, Dada artist Huelsenbeck wrote what came to be the first Dada manifesto in the German language.

What did Expressionism want? It "wanted" something, that much remains characteristic of it. Dada wants nothing, Dada grows. Expressionism wanted inwardness, it conceived of itself as a reaction against the times, while Dadaism is nothing but an expression of the times ... Under the pretext of inwardness the Expressionist [artists] have closed ranks to form a generation which is expectantly looking forward to an honorable appraisal in the histories of art and literature and is aspiring to honors and accolades.

(Huelsenbeck and Green 1993: 44–5)

Mary Wigman maintained the Expressionist conviction that art could express an intrinsic human truth and thus restore meaning to people's lives. The Dadaists proclaimed that all extant moral, political and aesthetic beliefs had been destroyed by the war. The coolness and radicalism of the *Neue Sachlichkeit* and Dada developments do manifest themselves in Mary Wigman's use of mask and costume as a way of depersonalizing the performing body. But her themes remained essentially Expressionistic: ecstatic or somber and imbued with mysticism and symbolic imagery. Her primary allegiance to *Ausdruckstanz* would eventually place her at odds not only with Laban but also with larger political and artistic forces within Germany. However, remnants of her time with the Dada artists remained in the theatricality of her performances and the revolutionary way she used the mask and costume in modern concert dance.

On 18–19 August 1917, Laban and Wigman, along with others from Laban's dance group, returned to the mountains of Ascona. There they presented a twelve-hour, open-air performance of a *Sonnenfest* (Sun Festival). Termed by Laban a "choral play," the spectacle was part of the Congress of the Oriental Order of the Temple or **Ordo Templi Orientis**. Through studies with OTO founder Theodor Reuss, Laban had been initiated into that branch of Freemasonry and progressed to the highest degree of Reuss's renegade Masonic organization. Laban's stated goal was the "renunciation of all civilizational influences" (Laban 1975: 135). The festival began at 6 a.m. with the *Hymn to the Rising Sun*. The second act of the performance was sited around a fire on a mountaintop at 11 p.m. Involving the entire cast armed with flutes, drums and torches, *The Demons of the Night* section was "a mystical play in which 'witches and demons' were conjured up in masked dances" (ibid.: 22). Following the marathon event, Wigman returned with Laban to Zurich. Then in November she made her own evening, her first dramatic cycle, built of solo dances performed at the Laban School. The six dances that made up the program reflected her fascination with the mystical and the metaphysical. *The Nun*, *The Dancer for Our Blessed Lady*, *Worshiper*, *Sacrifice*, *The Dervish* and *The Temple Dance* did not emerge merely from her experiences with Laban but reveal an atmosphere that permeated the place and time.

Ordo Templi Orientis – secret, mystical fraternity founded around 1902 by Karl Kellner and Theodor Reuss. Rudolf von Laban became a member of Reuss's renegade Masonic organization and brought the OTO to Monte Verità in 1917.

The longing for alternatives to the Western canon took some artists toward alternative spiritual teachings. The yin–yang symbol that stood atop the *Festhalle* at Hellerau represented a larger inquiry into aesthetic practices that similarly guided the work of **Wassily Kandinsky**, Franz Kafka, W.B. Yeats, T.S. Eliot and Mary Wigman. In film, Paul Wegener presented three versions of the ancient Golem story between 1915 and 1920. In 1919, Robert Weine directed the *Cabinet of Dr. Caligari*, the signature work of Expressionist film and a representation of the darker side of Expressionism through its thematic probing of insanity. The authors intended the tyranny of Dr. Caligari to serve as an allegory against mad authority, but the final version ends with the doctor telling his peers that he can cure his patient now that he understands the root of his own psychosis. Presentation of alternative realities became popular thematic material. For Wigman, such themes came to make a cohesive whole of her life and her work.

Wassily Kandinsky (1866–1944) – Russian abstract painter who was a leader of *Die Blaue Reiter* wing of German expressionism. His influential book *Concerning the Spiritual in Art* appeared in 1911. He became a German citizen upon joining the faculty of the Bauhaus school but was forced to leave the country in 1933 when the school was closed. He became a naturalized French citizen in 1939.

THE CRISIS YEAR

In 1918, Mary Wigman would have her own year of crisis, mental breakdown and self-analysis. The confusion and dissolution at war's end brought defeat, deprivation and desperation to the general population of Germany. Wigman experienced these and also was faced with difficulties in her personal life. In May, her stepfather Dietrich Wiegmann died and her brother Heinrich returned from the war as an amputee. Work at the studio in Zurich ended and Wigman also broke from her relationship with Laban. She found herself physically exhausted and emotionally drained. She went to a sanatorium at Walensee in eastern Switzerland to find some peace. She was also diagnosed with tuberculosis. In those days such a diagnosis could amount to a death sentence. In her writing, she refers to this period as a terrible, wonderful year. She danced alone and created a new series of solos. She also wrote the poetic sketches that were to become her group work *The Seven Dances of Life* (*Die Sieben Tanze des Lebens*) in 1921. Finally, she performed her dances at the sanatorium in Davos where the audience was made up of shell-shocked veterans, psychiatric patients and local sportsmen (Müller 1986a: 55). She was then ready to enter into a professional life.

After the Davos performance, she embarked on a tour of German cities, meeting disappointment at first as audiences were not prepared for her dances depicting the mysterious and the grotesque. What she presented onstage was a far cry from the beauty of ballet or the entertainment of the chorus line. Her first concerts in Berlin and Munich were critical debacles. Newspapers responded with cries of "ridiculous," "idiotic," "mad frenzy," "an imbecilic dislocation of the joints," "the dance without music – unbearable, fatiguing," "the drum and gong accompaniment (was) ear-splitting, torturous" (Dixon 1931: 37). Buffeted by these storms, Wigman did not surrender; nor did she change course. She persisted in her vision of *Ausdruckstanz* and finally in Hamburg the tide turned. She received her first real acclaim from the concert-going public.

When she continued on to Dresden, her audience had been well prepared by art historian and dance aficionado Will Grohmann. With Grohmann's help, Wigman, joined by dancers **Berthe Trümpy** and **Grete Palucca**, danced to a sold-out house. On 7 November, six days before her thirty-fifth birthday, newspaper critic Otto Flake wrote, "She realized an idea and fulfilled her task. Dance is for her a religious art" (Müller 1986a: 71). This early success in Dresden was the beginning of a long, fruitful relationship with that city.

Berthe Trümpy (1895–1983) – studied with both Wigman and Laban. She helped finance the first Mary Wigman Schule-Dresden. Trümpy became co-director of the school, teaching and performing with the Chamber Dance Group. In 1926, along with Vera Skoronel, she started the Trumpy/Skoronel school in Berlin.

Gret Palucca (1902–93) – was a student at the Dresden Opera House when she saw a Wigman performance. She began to study at the Wigman Schule. Identified by her gift for high jumps, Palucca was considered one of the most talented of Wigman's dance progeny. Palucca stayed in Germany during the Third Reich and gained a favored position even though she was defined under the Nuremberg Laws as *mischlinge ersten Grades*, or half Jewish. Her school in East Germany became an important training ground for postwar German dancers.

Meanwhile, the Weimar government was convulsed in one political upheaval after another. Caught on tour during the Kapp-Putsch and the ensuing general strike, she hitched a ride to Dresden and in many ways her fate was decided there. Wigman writes that in 1920 she was to be engaged by the Dresden State Opera as ballet master. She moved to the Palast Hotel Weber with Trümpy, who had become her assistant, to await her appointment. While there, Wigman began to teach classes in the hotel social room. From a newspaper article, she learned that the position at the Opera had passed her by, awarded to another who had influential romantic connections. Undeterred, Wigman continued to teach in the hotel; many students came but there seemed to be no resolution of Wigman's dream for a center in which to train dancers and from which to take her own creative performance work out into the world. Finally, Berthe Trümpy took action and, using her own Swiss francs, acquired a villa for Wigman in Neustadt-Dresden. It would be the primary home of the Wigman School for the next twenty-two years.

THE GILDED AND TARNISHED TWENTIES

Later in her life, Wigman would reflect on the 1920s as a "fighting time" of hard and relentless work. But she acknowledged that the end of the First World War brought a surge of creative activity in all of the arts. Much has been written of the inspired swell of innovation that was unleashed in spite of, or perhaps in response to, the ongoing political disarray that plagued the Weimar Republic. Not only was the political situation in flux, but also the economic conditions were equally unsettled. Yet Mary Wigman's school flourished. A roll-call of the students who came to study with Wigman in the 1920s reads like a list of the most important professional dancers of the era. Along with Trümpy, Grete Palucca, **Yvonne Georgi**, **Harald Kreutzberg**, **Max Terpis**,

Margarethe Wallmann and **Hanya Holm** all came to work with Wigman at the house on Bautzner Strasse in the early 1920s. As Wigman's workload grew, she was able to enlist help from several sources.

Yvonne Georgi (1903–75) – born in Leipzig, she attended the Dalcroze school in Hellerau. In 1921 Georgi went to the Wigman school in Dresden. Her successful partnership with Harald Kreutzberg took the duo on tour across Europe and to the United States of America.

Harald Kreutzberg (1902–68) – student of Wigman at the Dresden school who became one of the great soloists of his era. Equally renowned as a dancer and actor, he worked with Max Terpis and Max Reinhardt. In 1928 he traveled to the United States as a member of Max Reinhardt's theater group and returned to the States for the next seven years with Yvonne Georgi and with American dancer Ruth Page as his partners.

Max Terpis (1889 – 1958) – early student of Mary Wigman, Terpis taught at the Wigman school. He became ballet master in Hanover in 1922.

Hanya Holm (1893–1992) – Wigman student who became her teaching assistant and started the American Wigman School. Holm was also a graduate of the Dalcroze Institute. She eventually became a successful Broadway choreographer with such shows as *My Fair Lady*, *Kiss Me Kate* and *Camelot* to her credit. She was the first to bring Mary Wigman's ideas to the United States.

At age twenty-seven, Mary's sister Elisabeth was still living with their mother in Hanover. In 1921, she came to join Mary's household in Dresden. While their mother had warned her not to take up the dance, she started in Trümpy's evening class for amateurs. Eventually, Elisabeth would take on a great deal of the teaching and day-to-day responsibilities at the school. The same year, the accomplished musician

Will Goetz joined the faculty and began to serve as Wigman's collaborator for her dance compositions. With Goetz, she was able to further
develop her ideas about the relationship between music and the dance.
She also made use of the dancers that she had gathered around her to
create group works, including her dance drama *The Seven Dances of Life*.
Choreographing that work in 1921, she broke from the solo performances that had defined the previous four years of her career.

As her reputation as a teacher and performer grew, so did the
enrollment of her school. Soon students were coming from far beyond
Germany to study her new dance. The dressing room has often been
described as a place where many languages could be heard. In Germany,
Ausdruckstanz became popular among the citizens of the Weimar
Republic who were hungry for a life-affirming physical culture.
Participation in rhythmic gymnastics and *Ausdruckstanz* became a mass
movement, alongside the movement choir explorations of Rudolf von
Laban and the hiking clubs of the German Youth Movement.

By 1923, Germany was experiencing a measure of economic stability that was mirrored in Wigman's personal life and work. The city of
Dresden was able to contribute some financial support to her concert
dance group. Her school was flourishing and her choreography was
reaching a new level of professionalism. Since her days at Hellerau,
Wigman had enjoyed a friendship that grew into a romantic relationship with psychiatrist **Hans Prinzhorn**. Prinzhorn's work concerned
the common ground between psychiatry and art, irrationality and
self-expression. In 1922 Prinzhorn published his first and most influential book, *Bildnerei der Geisteskranken* (*Artistry of the Mentally Ill*),
richly illustrated with examples from his collection of artwork by
mental patients. This book represents one of the first attempts to
clinically analyze and value such work. Wigman found that she had many
ideas in common with Prinzhorn, who was a strong influence in her
philosophical and aesthetic thinking as well as her domestic life. The
two remained friends even after the romance ended; after his death
in 1933, Wigman kept a death mask of Prinzhorn in her home for
many years. And he helped to form that home in ways beyond his
lifetime. In his Heidelberg practice, Prinzhorn had employed Anni
Hess as assistant and housekeeper. As Wigman's school and performing
career flourished, she was able to ask "Hesschen" to manage her domestic
affairs. Hess would remain a devoted companion to the dancer from
1923 until Wigman's death in 1973. Indeed, a good portion of the

story of Wigman's life lies with the devotion of her housekeeper and companion, Anni Hess.

Hans Prinzhorn (1886–1933) – German psychiatrist and art historian whose work at the University of Heidelberg was concerned with the border between art and psychiatry, self-expression and mental illness. He was Mary Wigman's lover, confidant and companion during her early years in Dresden.

With the assistance of her students, accompanists, sister Elisabeth and Hess, plus financial support from private donors, the city of Dresden, the Saxon state and the federal government, Wigman entered into a period of tremendous productivity. By 1924, she was able to expand her professional group to fourteen dancers. She also became involved with a man fifteen years younger. **Herbert Binswanger** was from a well-known Swiss family of physicians and psychiatrists. His own specialty was also psychotherapy and he provided a boyish and light-hearted diversion for Wigman, in contrast to her student/pupil role with Prinzhorn. Her time with Binswanger served to further free her as she came into her own as an artist.

Herbert Binswanger (1901–1975) – member of the great family of psychiatrists that founded and operated Bellevue Sanatorium in Kreuzlingen, Switzerland. His uncle Otto had treated Friedrich Nietzsche during his illness. His father Ludwig trained with Jung and had a close relationship with Freud. Ludwig also studied the writings of Heidegger and incorporated these ideas into his branch of existential psychology. Herbert also followed in the family avocation. After her relationship with Prinzhorn, Wigman began a romantic involvement with Herbert. Their correspondence and friendship lasted until her death.

Nearing her fortieth year, Wigman also was reaching a zenith in her creative development. She began to incorporate the use of the mask into her compositions, admitting what she would term an "alien figure" into the choreography. In 1926, she revisited the figure of the

Figure 5 Mary Wigman playing in Badensee. Photographer unknown, courtesy Tanzarchiv Berlin

witch, donning a mask to craft her second version of *Hexentanz*, a shocking study in female power and the grotesque. Paradoxically, the popularity of *Ausdruckstanz* had unleashed a whole population of earnest, emotive amateurs that threatened to undermine the professionalism of the art form. In the United States of America, Lincoln Kirstein would call Mary Wigman a dangerous woman because she encouraged all young women to dance, whether they had talent or not! The emerging debate between amateur and professional dance would continue into the next decade and would serve as a flash point for the field. As competing camps struggled for philosophical and aesthetic authority over dwindling resources, Wigman entered gamely into the fray.

THE FIRST DANCERS' CONGRESS

In December 1926, Germany was admitted to the League of Nations and began experiencing a sense of renewal, primarily orchestrated by foreign minister Gustav Stresemann and due partly to the reduction of war reparations under the Treaty of Locarno. Stresemann declared to the Geneva Assembly:

> He will serve humanity best who, firmly rooted in the traditions of his own people, develops his moral and intellectual gifts to the best of his ability, thus reaching out beyond his own national boundaries and serving the whole world.
> (Stresemann in Reinhardt 1962: 666)

Wigman shared Stresemann's goal of creating a German art that would spread beyond the country's borders. The First Dancers' Congress took place at Magdeburg in May 1927, with the goal of assembling leading German dancers to discuss the most pressing issues of their time. Attendance was modest, around three hundred people, and Laban and his supporters dominated the proceedings. At the Congress, Laban put forward his desire to unite all German dance organizations in a single federation, ostensibly under his own leadership. Wigman and her own disciples stayed away from the primary activities of the conference since Laban had not invited Wigman to participate in the concert performances.

During the Congress, the *Magdeburg Daily News* invited both Laban and Wigman to contribute to a special issue devoted to the German theater. Laban wrote "The Dance as a Work of Art," offering new

approaches to movement for the stage in what appeared to be a recon-
ciliation of commercial theater, ballet and opera with his explorations
of group performance and movement choirs. With no other platform
from which to express her opinion at the Congress, Wigman used her
newspaper article as an opportunity to raise issues facing modern
dance and the dancer, as well as charges of dilettantism that had been
leveled at the *Ausdruckstanz*. On the defensive, Wigman delineated two
types of creative dance: the first was her own Absolute concert form
that reflected contemporary life and concerns; the second was what
she termed "stage dance," which she described as being in a state of
confusion and compromise between classical dance and pantomime.

Wigman argued that very few German stages had resident troupes
fully trained in the relatively young dance form of *Ausdruckstanz*. She
added that the young dancers of the day came from many strata of
society rather than those privileged enough to study ballet. In the
difficult economic climate of 1927 she asked, "Which dancers can
afford to finish their studies?" (Wigman 1973: 114). In comparing the
stage choreographer to the musical composer of the day, Wigman
declared that very few choreographers had the needed experience to
fully employ *Ausdruckstanz* on the theatrical stage. Hers was a plea for
patience to allow the development of the art form. In sum, Wigman,
Laban and other Congress participants could all agree that a crisis in
training had become obvious in the world of professional dance.
However, she and Laban would continue to disagree about the pre-
scription to remedy the situation.

THE SECOND DANCERS' CONGRESS

The Second Dancers' Congress was held in Essen in 1928. While rivalry
had flared between Wigman and Laban at the first Congress, Laban had
formed several alliances, most notably with his former student and
assistant **Kurt Jooss**. After leaving Laban, Jooss had established the
Folkwang School with Sigurd Leeder in Essen and was emerging as a fine
young choreographer. Jooss was also making his own claim as a leader
in the German dance and his role as organizer of the Second Congress
firmly established this position. Both men called for the integration
of classical ballet with the new dance modernism to create a unique
theatrical form. Although Wigman was invited to participate in this
Second Congress, she remained a rebel against what she termed

"hidebound conventional theater." She continued to call for the support of Absolute dance first and foremost as a foundation for more specialized work in theatrical productions. It is crucial to understand that she saw *Ausdruckstanz* as a primary, initiating base of experience for the dance artist. She claimed that it was the only form to assure freedom for individual development through improvisational methods rather than codified technique. Spotlighting the distance between Laban/Jooss and Wigman, the central question appeared to be: Did the future of dance lie with the *Ausdruckstanz*, which repudiated classical ballet altogether, or with the dance-drama which incorporated aspects of ballet as championed by Jooss and Laban's expressive movement methods to create a new entity?

Kurt Jooss (1901–79) – born in a village near Stuttgart to a farming family of landed gentry. Jooss encountered Laban in 1919 as he was working on theories of *Choreutics* and then joined *Tanzbühne Laban*. After traveling to Paris to study ballet, Jooss was awarded the 1932 Paris choreographic prize for his classic *The Green Table*. In 1933 Jooss was forced to flee Germany with his dance company and settled at Dartington Hall in England.

As economic tension grew, the practical possibility of paid work in the opera house or theater informed much of the discussion. For many dancers such work appeared to be the only option for economic sustenance. Notably, a similar debate was a large part of the climate of the US dance community during the Depression as many modern "concert" dancers would turn to what they termed commercial work: entertaining on the Broadway stage or under the auspices of the Works Project Administration. For the German dance world, the Second Congress displayed a discomfort and stagnation that had overtaken the field as well as the paralysis that had overtaken German society as factions battled for control on the political front. Karl Toepfer points out that during the conference very little attention was paid to aesthetic questions; the focus was on pedagogic concerns and career maneuvers. Laban did emerge as the leader once again, mostly based on the strength of his written work as a theoretical foundation for the artists. The press was particularly keen on the introduction of his *Kinetographie Laban* as the most comprehensive form of dance notation to date. Also, dance writer Hans Brandenburg commented that Laban had freed contemporary dance from Wigman's type of "excessive individualism" by choreographing choric works and creating a structure of uniformity through his theoretical writings and notation. To many observers, the Congress appeared long on talk and short on actual performance at the professional level.

However, Mary Wigman did dominate the conference in the one area closest to her own ideals and career goals. If critical reviews are the measure, the performance of her group work *Feier* (Celebration/Ceremony) was by far the best-received dance event of the conference. Using her well-trained group as abstractly stylized, even archetypal figures and rejecting narrative, she reiterated in dance form her belief that the future lay in revival of the ritual origins of dance, not assimilation of ballet or other theatrical forms. Aside from the rhetoric, the performance of *Celebration* solidified her prominence and mastery as a choreographer and supported her claim for the power of *Ausdruckstanz*. As a sad epilogue to the actual performance, Wigman appeared onstage and addressed the audience. She announced that due to financial difficulties she was forced to dissolve her dance group. The performance of *Celebration* was the end of an era.

It also proved to be the beginning of the next phase of her work. Wigman overcame the anxieties over the solvency and management of the school with the entry of industrialist **Hanns Benkert** into her life. Benkert had been involved romantically with Hanya Holm and through her had a good understanding of the problems facing the Wigman enterprise. An accomplished businessman, Benkert took over management of the school, allowing Wigman to breathe a sigh of relief.

Hanns Benkert (1899–1948) – director of the Society of German Engineers and a leading functionary in munitions production, he became manager of the Siemens Schuckert Works under the Third Reich.

THE THIRD DANCERS' CONGRESS

There was no German Dancers' Congress in 1929. As the global Depression began, Wigman had regained her equilibrium in spite of the disappointment that had followed the dissolution of her dance group. Following an idyllic road trip back to the Alps with old flame Binswanger, she returned to the studio to choreograph her solo dance cycle *Shifting Landscape*, which she was soon to premiere during her first tour of the United States. Wigman was assigned the most prominent choreographic project in the Third Dancers' Congress at Munich in 1930. This Congress was held under the auspices of three organizations: *Der Deutsche Tanzerbund* led by Laban and Jooss; *Deutsche Tanzgemeinschaft*, which Wigman established after the slight of the First Dancers' Congress; and the Munich *Chorische Bunde*, organized to supply amateur dancers for the production of Wigman's monumental dance-drama *Totenmal* or *Call of the Dead*. In the midst of economic hardships, the city of Munich renovated a concert hall to house performances, lectures and discussions. The eyes of the Western dance world were turned toward Germany in expectation. International newspapers sent correspondents. Elizabeth Selden's preview expressed the enthusiastic anticipation among US dancers. "For the third time Germany is calling a dance Congress and thereby proclaiming her great interest in the art of motion which is destined like no other, to express the consciousness of our modern age ..." (Selden 1930: n.p.).

The Congress promised to gather the largest group of dancers ever assembled and more than a thousand came. Many saw the Congress as proof of the profound importance of dance in the modern world. To disciples of the new dance, the magnitude of the event testified how dance had become "a potent factor in the cultural life of the age" (ibid.). The crowning event of the week was to be an open rehearsal of Wigman's *Totenmal*. Designed on a mass scale, *Totenmal* was written and directed by the young Swiss poet Albert Talhoff as a memorial for the dead of the First World War. Selden placed it in the tradition of the grand crucifixion re-enactment produced at Oberammergau. She described *Totenmal* as "the greatest Passion Play of the present, since every spectator here is an actor and has been since 1914 [when the war began]" (ibid.).

In reality, the entire Third Dancers' Congress was judged a disappointment. *New York Times* critic John Martin, the staunchest supporter of the modern dance on both sides of the Atlantic, called it "futile." Not only did he find the performances and presentations unsatisfactory, but also he was shocked at the state of contention within the dance community: "Invective was hurled about promiscuously, scandal was voiced and libel uttered; the private lives of individuals present were attacked and cries of 'Pfui!' and even 'Schwein!' – an epithet of untranslatable venom – filled the air" (Martin 1930: *New York Times*, 27 July, X6). This is how the Third Dancers' Congress closed: in an unseemly display of deep rifts within the German dance world.

Martin also wrote that the ambitious but flawed *Totenmal* had occupied Wigman to such an extent that she presented "no dancing of her own during the Congress, much to its detriment" (Martin 1930: *New York Times*, 27 July, X6). To Martin, *Totenmal* was an anomaly or diversion from Wigman's own work. But *Totenmal* was to be performed throughout the summer, with Wigman and her Dresden faculty remaining in residence in Munich.

The high expectations for the *Totenmal* performance reflected the hard-earned prominence that Wigman had gained in a German dance world that had grown increasingly impoverished, contentious and openly hostile. Wigman's own solo performances and touring had always been an important source of professional pride and income. By the end of 1930, she was about to embark on the most important touring cycle of her career.

COMING TO THE UNITED STATES

In the early 1930s, the person most responsible for the flowering of international dance in the United States was not a dancer. Sol Hurok was an impresario of the old school who presented acts across the country, most notably the early, exhaustive touring of Anna Pavlova and Isadora Duncan. He redoubled his efforts in the 1930s. The march of US big business in the first decades of the twentieth century also stormed through the field of art and entertainment. Corporations such as the National Broadcasting Company and the Columbia Broadcasting System overtook smaller presenters. Hurok intensified his self-proclaimed mission to remain an independent producer of "the interesting, the exotic, the novel from abroad." The opening of what Hurok came to call the "dance decade" began in 1930 with Mary Wigman (Hurok and Goode 1946: 155).

Certainly, the United States had its own dance ancestry. Isadora Duncan got her start there, as had Loie Fuller and **Ruth St. Denis**, although all had to travel to the European continent for major artistic success. **Martha Graham**, **Doris Humphrey** and Charles Weidman, all the offspring of Denishawn, were beginning to make a mark in the

Figure 6 *Totenmal*, 1930. Photographer unknown, courtesy of the Tanzarchiv Leipzig

cultural world and by 1930 were the rising stars in the rather small cosmos of American dance modernity. A 1927 *New York Times* article underscores the state of the dance prior to Wigman's arrival. It begins: "The advent of the new German 'physical culture' dancing in to the arena, though yet almost unknown in this country, is causing something to happen in the dance world." The writer goes on to describe a "blood feud" between the advocates and opponents of the ballet. Noting the significance of the fact that the "non-ballet" had not yet acquired a name, the writer tries a few, "esthetic, barefoot, interpretative, rhythmic," arguing that in the dance style itself there is little definitive enough to even bear a name. However, the writer offers hope: "Then, of course, there are the Germans. We have seen almost nothing of them as yet in this country, but Mary Wigman is reported to be headed in our direction." It would be three years before Wigman could make the voyage across the Atlantic. But her reputation preceded her and much preparation for her arrival was made through the work of John Martin. It is telling that the 1927 article bears no byline. This was not unusual. The identification of writer by byline was a fairly new addition to American journalism. There was no staff writer dedicated to the dance art at that time. In 1928, Martin was hired by the *Times* to do just that, launching his decades-long dominance of the field in the United States of America.

Ruth St. Denis (1880–1972) – with Ted Shawn, founded the Denishawn School in Los Angeles in 1915. Known as a striking soloist of "ethnic" styles in the first decade of the twentieth century, St. Denis went on to create "music visualizations" that wedded music to movement, arguably a development of Dalcroze's theories. At Denishawn she taught the American modern dance pioneers Martha Graham, Charles Weidman and Doris Humphrey.

Martha Graham (1894–1991) – seen by many as the founder of American modern dance, Graham codified a unique style and technique for dance which has been transmitted through her school, choreography and company.

Doris Humphrey (1895–1958) – contemporary of Graham and likewise an alumnus of Denishawn, Humphrey along with **Charles Weidman (1901–1975)** established a strain of American modern dance. Her use of the swing or fall and recovery has remained a mainstay as it has evolved in the art form. She was astute analyst of choreographic principles and her *The Art of Making Dances* (1959) became a bible for modern choreographers. Stricken early in life with debilitating arthritis, Humphrey continued to choreograph for **José Limón** and his company.

In January 1929, two students of Mary Wigman debuted their work in New York. Harald Kreutzberg and Yvonne Georgi had left the Wigman schools for careers as soloists and were now performing as a duo. They made their way to the United States before their teacher. Following their premiere, Martin was pressed to answer the question, "Is this the new German dance?" (Martin 1929: 29 January, X8). Martin's response displayed his tireless effort to educate the public on the dance revolution that was underway: "It is a complete restatement of physical technique, going back to nature and away from art for its experimentations. It also lays great stress on expressionism" (Martin 1929: 29 January, X8). As correspondent to the Third Dancers' Congress, Martin traveled to Germany in early August 1930. Finally, he was able to write definitively,

> When one comes face to face with Mary Wigman, the truth about the German dance dawns with unexpected suddenness; Mary Wigman is the German dance. ... the mystery of the German dance itself clears away in her presence.
> (Martin 1930: *New York Times*, 3 August, 101)

Wigman arrived in the United States in November. Hurok had booked her for a "scratch tour." Unsure of her appeal to American audiences, he added concert dates in response to demand. He needn't have worried. With great anticipation, the audiences paid her an unusual tribute. New York's Chanin Theater was completely sold out for her opening performance before she even left Germany! While exciting, this also laid upon her a tremendous sense of responsibility and even anxiety as she considered the task of bringing the "free dance" to an entirely new audience. The stage fright that plagued her all her life came roaring to the fore. Yet, as the curtain opened on that broad New York stage, she was greeted with a thunderous applause, a welcome that she would recall until her death. From her premiere in December, she was met by full houses, along with equal measures of enthusiastic support, perplexity and some outright dismay. Before her first tour, there was rumor that she would be forced to temper her program for consumption by the uninformed American public. Although John Martin pointed out that the homegrown American dancers such as Graham had already struggled mightily to introduce dance modernism, there was some doubt as to the sophistication and depth of the American public when faced with Wigman's unique theatricality. Uncompromising, for her first tour Wigman performed the same program that she had staged in Berlin and Hamburg just prior to her journey.

By her fourth performance, Martin claimed that undoubtedly a new epoch for dancing was beginning in the United States. Comparing the poetry of her movement to the nobility of Homer and the passion of Whitman, he continued, "it matters very little, if at all, that Frau Wigman herself is not possessed of personal beauty ..." (Martin 1931: *New York Times*, 4 January, X4). Not only was Wigman described as "past her prime," but also her concerts offered works that ruptured the tradition of classic beauty in the dance. Just as the crisis of the First World War brought into question the very relevance of beauty and order in a world radically altered by death and disfigurement, modernism in all of the arts had redefined art itself. Martin observed that Wigman brought to the surface aesthetic differences that had been stirring for years. Unquestionably, the authority and success of Wigman's work smoothed the path for the American moderns. Reflecting the development of a particular kind of Americana based on atavistic themes, Martha Graham choreographed *Primitive Rituals* and Doris Humphrey made *The Shakers*, both in 1931. That same year interest in the new German dance proved great enough that Hurok backed the establishment of an American Wigman School in New York, headed by Hanya Holm.

When Wigman returned to New York for her second tour in December 1931, Martin observed, "where there was curiosity and shocked surprise; now there is solid enthusiasm based on mutual understanding." (Martin 1931: *New York Times*, 14 December, X17). Wigman criss-crossed the country, remaining in North America for several months. Her solo dance cycle *Opfer* (*Sacrifice*) anchored her performances. In an interview, Wigman explained that she understood the enormous sacrifices that gripped the American public in the Great Depression. At the climax of the Depression, thirty million were unemployed worldwide, including six million in Germany alone. Wigman also noted that while she herself had not been adversely affected, largely due to the economic success of her American tours, many in her homeland were suffering deprivation. In spite of the economy, she performed for full houses. Hurok was no longer unsure of Wigman's ability to draw a crowd.

She crossed the country to perform for audiences on the West Coast. In San Francisco, young dancer **Eve Gentry** sat in the audience. Gentry later would join Hanya Holm's original dance group in New York. But for her introduction to Mary Wigman, she was another uninitiated audience member. And her response offers a glimpse of Wigman's impact on the American public. With notebook in hand, Eve recorded her impressions of her first contact with Mary Wigman's *Ausdruckstanz*. She wrote, "I will not let [others] influence me in my reactions, tho' they are over enthusiastic I will not be so until I am sure, sure that I want to give this enthusiasm to Mary Wigman" (Newhall 2000: 36). By the end of the concert, Gentry's restraint dissolved into unabashed admiration.

> I've been sitting on the edge of my seat, my knee quivering. I feel as tho' I just can't sit here longer – I must jump up. I feel as if I have seen a great artist. I have a great deal to think about, a great deal to dance for. I have actually learned things. The audience was riotous. People yelled "Bravo!" "Bravo." I have never been in such an excited place. I have never been so excited it seems. For the first time in my life I wanted to call "Bravo" so much that I actually did scream "Bravo" not only once but a dozen times, I was exhausted, trembling almost crying for joy.
>
> (Gentry papers)

Eve Gentry (1909–94) – American modern dancer, born Henrietta Greenhood. Studied with German dancer **Ann Mundstock** in San Francisco before becoming a member of Hanya Holm's original dance company in 1936. Gentry was also a member of the New Dance Group and was one of Joseph Pilates' chosen representatives.

DER WEG (THE PATH)

Wigman had succeeded in carrying the seeds of *Ausdruckstanz* across Europe and to the United States. She had caused a sensation and furthered her mission to spread the dance that she loved so well. The income and artistic interest generated from her tours allowed her to continue to expand her work and schools. In 1931, the American Wigman School was established with Hanya Holm at its helm. However, when Mary Wigman returned home in 1932, she once again found her German school in financial crisis. In Berlin alone 35,000 businesses were facing bankruptcy. The worldwide depression had thrown many of her students out of work. With massive unemployment, very few could pay tuition for the professional training program and even enrollment in the lay classes dropped precipitously. The struggle for state funds grew even more difficult. She had turned over financial administration of her school to Hanns Benkert, whose successful business ventures had him attached to the Siemens Corporation. He was also well connected politically with the rising National Socialist Party, as German industry threw support to the Nazis. For Wigman, his business acumen and political protection became invaluable as she struggled to retain her school and continued a relentless cycle of touring her solo concerts to keep the school afloat.

In July of 1932, Hurok came to Berlin and approached Wigman about a third US tour. The offer appeared a godsend. She hatched a plan to use the tour to raise the profile of her school, employing and thus retaining some of her more advanced students. This could only serve to build future support for her enterprise. She would start a new dance group with these advanced students and create a major new work for them. The new Wigman Dance Group would tour the United States from coast to coast and into Canada. The group would not only be paid for travel and performances, it would also be paid to rehearse, and not in falling Deutschmarks but in solid American dollars, a development that caused much excitement within the Wigman school community (Müller 1986a: 212). She even talked with Hurok about an extended tour to South America.

Once more, Hurok kept all plans contingent on audience enthusiasm, again placing Wigman under extreme pressure to produce. She had less than six months to pull together a group of students who had never performed professionally into an elite troupe equal to an international tour and to make a work that highlighted her own theories of the group dance. She wrote in frustration of the great goodwill of the girls and their equally naive view of the hard work necessary to accomplish such a feat (ibid.). The Group unveiled her new dance cycle *Der Weg* (The Way/Path) on 8 December 1932, in Dresden and performed it again three days later in Berlin (ibid.). They met with sharp disapproval in the press. Leading critics Fritz Böhme and Paul Bloch both challenged Wigman's choice of the group form instead of her own, much stronger solo work. Unaware of the necessities that shaped Wigman's choices, or perhaps in spite of them, Böhme declared it regrettable that this work would represent the current state of German dance and claimed it a greater shame that the work must travel directly to the United States without correction of the problems evident in the German performances. The criticism was surely searing to Wigman, who was feeling pressures from all directions. Perhaps the most painful of all proved to be the assertions that the great Mary Wigman had become artistically and spiritually lost, deserting the values of her homeland (ibid.: 213).

When Wigman arrived for her third US tour in mid-December 1932, she was not alone. Along with accompanists Hanns Hasting and Gretl Curth, she brought those twelve student dancers to perform *Der Weg*. The hurtful claims that dilettantism was making *Ausdruckstanz* obsolete appeared proven. In the case of *Der Weg*, practical necessity prevailed. In the world of concert performance, the proof is what happens onstage. And competition in the United States was heating up. Graham, Humphrey and Weidman all had cast well away from their Denishawn roots. Their own concert aesthetics were evolving and their own schools had growing enrollments.

The American debut of *Der Weg* took place on Christmas Day at the New Yorker Theatre. Wigman was given the opening-night spot of a two-week International Dance Festival. John Martin, ever a champion of Wigman's work, wrote kindly: "Twelve excellently trained dancers, able to alternate between movement and the playing of flutes and percussion instruments, constitute the company" (Martin 1932: *New York Times*, 26 December, 26). He goes on to try to describe the relationship between Wigman and her dancers in the work, "among them Wigman herself moves as the protagonist, though not actually the most important figure." He does concede that "Wigman with a group is not to be compared with Wigman as a solo dancer" (ibid.).

Indeed, Martin and others who had come that evening to see the power of Wigman seemed sorely disappointed that she had made herself an auxiliary of the group, rather than the focus. This was a departure even from her earlier choric staging of *Totenmal*, in which she was the only unmasked, individual figure. Martin claimed that no fault lay in her composition: Wigman was a stickler for clear form, but she had chosen to discard her strongest artistic tool – her own performance personality. Martin saw clearly that:

> Her singular power as an artist lies in her ability to project her highly personal inner experience through movement of sometimes breath-taking originality. When she gives these movements to other dancers, she runs the risk of making them appear manufactured and unconvincing.
>
> (ibid.)

In letters, Wigman recorded this difficult beginning of the tour. During the seven New York performances shouts came from the audience, "Mary Wigman Solo!" (Müller 1986a: 214). This certainly didn't aid the confidence of the younger dancers although Wigman did claim a victory in their Chicago performance to a nearly full house (ibid.). The tour was originally planned to take the group by bus and train to Cincinnati, Louisville, Chicago, Winnipeg, Calgary, Vancouver, Seattle, San Francisco, Oakland, Los Angeles, Pasadena, San Diego, Salt Lake City, Denver, Kansas City, Tulsa, Denton, St. Louis, Indianapolis and beyond (ibid.). By the time they reached San Francisco on 15 January, Wigman had inserted solo works from other dance cycles. It appeared an act of desperation, to tear apart the fabric of *Der Weg* with substitutions, sacrificing the subtle sense of the original evening with something that would please the crowd. Martin perceived that, just as Wigman had subordinated herself to the group, she had now been forced "into a mood and style lighter and less vital than her own" (Martin 1933: *New York Times*, 15 January, X2). Aside from Wigman's valiant attempts to fix the program, the tour had become a fiasco. There would be no South American leg. In fact Hurok declared he had had enough. Never one to back a losing proposition, he suggested that Wigman wait until 1934 or 1935 to return, when the public might be receptive to her work once again. She could no longer envision her future as a "New World" touring artist. By the time that Wigman made it back to New York for her farewell concert on 6 March, she had abandoned *Der Weg.* Instead she danced solo, primarily drawing on dances from the heroic *Opfer* (Sacrifice) cycle, along with *Allegro Arioso* from her *Spanish Suite* and *Monotonie Whirl* from the 1926 group work *Celebration* and *Summer's Dance*, the dances most loved by US audiences in her earlier tours (ibid.). It was a much lighter and more virtuosic program than *Der Weg.*

Perhaps American audiences had grown tired of the heavy expressionism that characterized *Der Weg*, perhaps they were developing a proprietary sense of aesthetic judgement raised by the increasing abilities of their homegrown dancers, or perhaps the young student dancers were just not up to the task. The xenophobia and anti-German sentiment that would come full blown with the rise of the Third Reich may have been partially responsible. When Sol Hurok wrote of that season in his 1946 memoir he put it this way: "One stocky Amazon, providing it was the miraculous Wigman herself, was all right, but a whole group of thick-waisted, thick-legged German girls in wide-skirted bathing suits was too much" (Hurok 1946: 161).

However, for her final US concert there was nothing but praise and admiration for Mary Wigman. Martin deemed her solo performance "of unusual brilliance," even judged by her own high standards (Martin 1933: *New York Times*, 6 March, 16). The audience filled the New Yorker Theatre to overflowing and "there was in the atmosphere that tension and enthusiasm which mark special occasions" (ibid.). Martin reported the next day that no one moved when the evening was over. Instead "flowers were thrown upon the stage and cheering and applause were maintained for more than a dozen curtain calls" (ibid.). Wigman responded with an encore of her *Gypsy Moods*. But the cheering continued and only an impromptu farewell speech by Wigman satisfied the crowd before the final curtain could fall. In many ways that final curtain call signaled the end of Wigman's brightest years. Hurok recalled:

> Mary Wigman strode down Broadway one evening in 1933 … It was late, after a performance, and the morning papers were out. That was the day of the last legal election in Germany. Wigman begged for the newspapers, and the lot of them hurried down the steps into Childs Restaurant in the Paramount Building basement to read the election returns. She was happy that night. The Hitler gang had been beaten.

> (Hurok 1946: 162)

In the elections of 6 November 1932, the National Socialists had lost thirty-five seats in the Reichstag, but this would change in less than three months.

RETURNING TO THE NEW GERMANY

By the time her boat docked in Germany, Mary Wigman's homeland was in paroxysms of change. She wrote in her daybook, "The new Germany – not simply a change of government but a Revolution – Strange!!! Where is it going?" (Wigman in Müller 1986a: 214). The Weimar government had suffered so many setbacks, creating a politic of instability that spanned economic, social and cultural life. Fear of communism galvanized support for reactionary right-wing elements, including the National Socialists. While Wigman was in the United States, a campaign was mounted to convince aging President von Hindenburg to name Hitler as Chancellor, both as an attempt at uni-fication and to appease conservative elements. Hitler did become Chancellor on 30 January 1933, but he by no means took absolute control at that time. The Nazis promoted the myth of the *Machtergreifung* (seizure of power). However, many still felt that Hitler could be contained and his popular support co-opted. Between 1933 and 1934 he methodically pursued his policy of *Gleichschaltung* (literally, bringing or forcing into line), strengthening his grip on German politics and expanding his reach into all cultural life, particularly the lives of German artists (Fulbrook 1991: 55).

Hitler's art program was not initiated abruptly, nor did it reach its full span all at once. With the gift of hindsight it is natural to question Mary Wigman's accommodations with the new regime. The love of her homeland runs strongly throughout her writings, speeches and creative work. The rise of nationalism was endemic in the twentieth-century West. In the United States, one can point to Martha Graham's promotional material and the choreography of her own Americana as another example of the nationalist impulse. That Wigman did not use her celebrity to speak out against the Third Reich once the evil core of the regime was revealed may represent the most authentic con-demnation of her choices. The question of why she chose to stay in Germany remains. Hedwig Müller underscores the fact that Wigman could never desert her homeland. She felt called to bring forth the new German dance with a profundity that equaled the art of Goethe,

Schiller and Nietzsche. For her, this was her destiny, the purpose of her life. It was *Schiksal* and *Opfer* – fate and sacrifice.

Historian Hellmut Lehmann-Haupt argues that each revolutionary change favors a brief experimental cooperation of politically and artistically radical forces. Such association seems to rest largely on mutual misunderstanding or hopeful projection, one obvious reason for its brevity. In his speech to open the Reich's Chamber of Culture in April 1933, **Joseph Goebbels** said, "Every genuine artist is free to experiment." The Depression of the early 1930s had exacerbated an already difficult economic situation. With much work, Wigman had kept her school afloat but most artists held a common conviction that fundamental structural reform of the arts would be required. This conviction underlay the strife within the dance community. Unsatisfactory administrative infrastructure was widely blamed for the lack of professionalism among the schools of dance and for the lack of adequate financial support for the arts or for pensions for artists. Wigman was one of the lucky ones, due to the profits from her American tours. With the less than successful final tour of *Der Weg*, the American source of income appeared closed. The Third Reich came in with a strong message of economic support for the German arts and further support for those great national artists such as Wigman. Those shaping the new Germany quickly grasped the public relations power of international stars like Mary Wigman.

Joseph Goebbels (1897–1945) – Adolf Hitler's Minister of Propaganda and Popular Enlightenment and director of the *Reichskulturkammer*, or Reich Chamber of Culture. He controlled the total output of the German media. He competed for cultural oversight with **Alfred Rosenberg (1893–1946)**, who was appointed in 1934 to the "Custodianship of the Entire Intellectual and Spiritual Training and Education of the Party and of All Coordinated Associations." Rosenberg was director of the Office of Racial Politics.

DANCING IN DRESDEN, 1933–1942

Dresden provided a home for Wigman's dance life over the longest period and greatest achievements of her extraordinary career. As the German dance was growing into an institution, Wigman was at the exciting and conflicted forefront of that growth. The contentiousness at the German Dancers' Congresses already reflected a systematic attempt by the Weimar government to regulate dance education even before the advent of the Third Reich. The studio schools were home to these developments, just as government regulation of art education had been going on long before the National Socialists came to power. It took nearly a year for the Saxon Ministry of Economics and the Dresden Board of Education to register Wigman's school as a legitimate vocational institution that could receive financial support and issue diplomas to professional students. And this was under the Weimar Republic. The survival of Wigman's school depended on such official recognition amid growing competition, economic depression and rising costs. Additionally, Wigman had to demonstrate that the school did not need student tuition to survive, that she had sufficient state and city support, as well as adequate income from her touring. Wigman had depended on public grants to support her dance groups, so changes in educational policies and public attitudes affected her school as well. Long merged, the studies of *Gymnastik* and artistic *Tanz* were officially separated by 1930. During the long absences for her international tours from 1930 to 1933, the city of Dresden was beset with rising unemployment and severe cuts in public welfare, school maintenance and other public services.

Gymnastik – movement as a means for physical training, relaxation and recreation, in contrast to **Tanz**, movement used for symbolic representation or communication through kinetic empathy.

Wigman observed the regime change in 1933 when she returned from her last extended American tour. She continued her relationship with Benkert. And while he eventually became prominent in the Nazi Party, Benkert was an established businessman, not a street thug or rabid brownshirt. And Wigman was no longer a young woman. Nearing fifty, she turned to him and he offered a sort of anchor, not unlike the stability of her early upbringing. At this time of crisis in her career and her homeland she returned physically and figuratively to her own roots. No longer the rebel artist, she was now established as the face of the great German dance. Her journal offers some small evidence of her reaction to the new government. Her letters to Hanya Holm during this period reveal even less. Wigman did recognize the Third Reich as a radical change from the beleaguered Weimar Republic, but her focus remained on her German career, particularly after the disappointments of her final overseas tour. She acted decisively to secure the continuation of her primary interests, her school, her dance group, her work.

The Third Reich's mergers of social, technical and political associations put an end to many schools and to the careers of teachers not already licensed. Diplomas from unaccredited schools were not honored, ending any chance of student income. Some schools sought to strengthen their positions as the new status quo took shape. In April 1933 the Law for Restoration of the Professional Civil Service enforced dismissals for those deemed insufficiently educated, politically unreliable or "non-Aryan." The same month, the Gestapo carried out a house search at the Wigman School based on suspicions of "communist machinations." At the same time, the passage of the Law Against Congestion of German Schools excluded Jewish pupils. Wigman fell under suspicion for many reasons. She had traveled abroad frequently and for long periods, she had Jewish dancers in her professional group and Jewish pupils whom she retained in her school, despite the law. The remodeling of her school in 1927 was partly funded by foreign capital and lists of communist party "agitators" included dancers certified by her school. Wigman was taken aback at the intrusion by the authorities. Hedwig Müller points out that in the end it was the detrimental effect of governmental interference upon her work that most outraged Wigman.

In July 1933, following the merger with the Palucca School and the Trümpy School, the *Wigman Schule Gruppe* joined the National Socialist Teachers Federation and opened new branches in Chemnitz, Erfurt, Hamburg, Hanover and Stuttgart. The government prescribed a new dance curriculum as Joseph Goebbels took over leadership of the **Reichskulturkammer**. Wigman appeared as guest lecturer at the *Deutsche Tanzbühne*. But already her motives were under government scrutiny. An anonymous document from the *Bundesarchiv*, dated 16 December 1934, states,

---

Reichskulturkammer – Reich's Chamber of Culture, established in 1933 promptly after Hitler became chancellor, under Joseph Goebbels, the minister of culture and popular enlightenment.

> … Can one consider a woman truly German, who only two years ago changed
> her name by deed poll from the good German Marie Wiegmann into the
> English form Mary Wigman? Besides it is very well known that the teaching
> personnel … in the Wigman School in Dresden and in Chemnitz is made up
> exclusively of communist-Bolsheviks and that the Jews play the main role in
> the school …
>
> (Karina and Kant 2004: 216)

What does such a letter mean? As an anonymous document, it is difficult to ascertain its direct impact but it does reflect the backbiting and infighting that were encouraged under the *Reichskulturkammer*. It also points to an atmosphere of growing fear and mistrust.

The same day that the accusing letter was filed, 16 December 1934, saw the closing of the German Dance Festival in Berlin. In their analysis of this Festival, David Buch and Hana Worthen point to "the discrepancy between the values embodied in National Socialist discourse and the values represented on the stage" (Buch and Worthen 2007: 216). The parameters of the "new German dance" also appear to have been fluid. Mary Wigman presented her *Frauentanzen* (Women's Dances) both as a new group work and as an excerpted solo within the four-day span of the festival. The sections in the dance suite were all themes that Wigman had addressed in earlier works. Susan Manning analyzes the *Women's Dances* as choreographic proof of Wigman's accommodations with National Socialist ideals. The dance was still essentially Expressionist. Program notes describe the dance as evoking "all five life-spheres of women's experience" and symbolizing her powers: girlish mirth (Wedding Dance), motherhood (Maternal Dance – a solo for Wigman), female capacity for suffering and grief (Lament for the Dead – a familiar theme), prophecy (Dance of the Prophetess) and the final section was a group *Hexentanz* (Witch Dance), subtitled "the abyss." Extant photos show a very animated and smiling group of young women and Wigman with arms akimbo as if throwing a spell outward and delighting in their "witchiness" (ibid.: 236)!

Meanwhile, in the United States Hanya Holm represented the Wigman School as one of the "Big Four" leaders of modern dance – along with Graham, Humphrey and Weidman – when the Bennington College program began in 1934. In parallel, as Roosevelt's economic recovery program established the Federal Theatre Project in the United States, dance in Germany came under the regulation of the Department of

Stage in the Reich Theater Chamber. A German dancers' constitution was drafted, including examinations and course guidelines. The 1935 Nuremberg Laws deprived the Jewish population and their spouses of citizenship rights and Wigman's long-time costume designer Elis Griebel was forced to emigrate in response. Wigman remained committed to her representation of the German dance and her first book, *Deutsche Tanzkunst* (1935), shows her determination to support the dance art of her homeland. The distance between Mary Wigman and her international peers had widened into an impassable chasm. Martha Graham declined an invitation to the International Dance Competition in July of 1936, implying that the Jewish members of her company would not be welcome in Germany. Responding to anti-German sentiment, Hanya Holm changed the name of the New York Wigman School to the Hanya Holm School, with Wigman's blessing, in 1936. As alliances formed among nations, they were also played out on a smaller scale among the dance dynasties.

Opening-night ceremonies of the 1936 Olympic Games in Berlin featured a pageant, *Olympic Youth*, produced by Hanns Niedecken-Gebhard. Along with Gret Palucca and Harald Kreutzberg, Mary Wigman danced in the newly constructed Olympic Stadium. Her *Lament for the Dead*, with music composed by **Carl Orff**, was choreographed and performed by Wigman supported by eighty female dancers (Partsch-Bergshon 1994: 92). Rudolf von Laban was to contribute a spectacle with a thousand dancers to the Olympic event, but when when Joseph Goebbels saw the rehearsal, he was appalled and wrote in his diary:

> Rehearsal of dance work: freely based on Nietzsche, a bad, contrived and affected piece. I forbid a great deal. It is so intellectual. I do not like it. That is because it is dressed up in our clothes and has nothing whatever to do with us.
>
> (Preston-Dunlop 1998: 196)

Carl Orff (1895–1982) – German composer and pedagogue and co-founder of the Guenther School for gymnastics, music and dance in Munich. In 1955, Wigman staged and choreographed productions of Orff's *Carmina Burana* and *Catulli Carmina* for the National Theatre Mannheim.

As the political reins tightened on the artists who had stayed in Germany, many began to realize their perilous state. At the Olympics, Wigman was presented for the last time as Germany's greatest dancer. Her diaries reveal her caught up in the task of that monumental ceremony dedicated to power, prestige and dominance. But soon she came to see that her name was used for a purpose far removed from highlighting the dance art. Within a year her new branch schools were eliminated and the *Wigman Schule Gruppe* was deleted from the National School Registry. She received no further subsidies. Meanwhile her accompanists Hanns Hasting and his wife Gretl Curth expanded their own range of influence within the Nazi Party, benefiting from Wigman's decline even as they remained in her Dresden school.

Wigman had proven too intellectual, too deep and too independent. Ultimately, Goebbels and other Party officials did not welcome her or her *Ausdruckstanz*. Under the National Socialists, dance had to be functional and deemed healthy, meaning angst-free, strong, goal-oriented, happy, *Volkish* and, most importantly, anti-intellectual. Wigman's dances were far from these things. Just as Hitler turned from his devotion to Wagner toward *The Merry Widow* operetta, artistic dance was to become entertainment providing diversion and depicting a particular version of popular history. Art criticism was banned, as was any art outside the Party line. Expressionism, essentially individualistic, unsettling and emotive, was dangerous. And Wigman was seen as a dangerous woman.

It was her artistic autonomy that caused her to hesitate when asked to contribute a dance in honor of Hitler, leading to the break between Wigman and the Party in May 1937. Her performance was to be part of the ceremonies inaugurating Munich's House of German Art, for which Hitler had laid the cornerstone in 1933. As a note, it is telling that the first official construction undertaken by the Nazis was this building dedicated to housing artworks. What became starkly clear by 1937 was that only a particular kind of artwork would be housed there. Albert Talhoff was in charge of the production and he first contacted Wigman. She wrote in her diary:

> The play!? [It is] Talhoff's invention even though there is obviously outside backing. [It is] *Totenmal* over and over again. Also the swinging flags are not absent. What makes me pensive and shaken and dismayed in my deepest being is the fact that the "artistic" [or dance] part of the play is only concerned

with the years following the First World War. The new time under the Third Reich should appear symbolically calm …

(Wigman in Müller 1986a: 244–5)

Hanns Hasting went as her representative to the initial planning meeting for the event. In her writing Wigman appears hard pressed between her ideals and official demands. Both Benkert and Hasting advised that she could not decline the invitation. She wrote that she had known this immediately with Talhoff's phone call. She likened the demands of this project to "Barbarism – indeed … a decline like that of Greek tragedy, a decline that brought the Roman pantomime. We experience the same decline." Her diary entries reveal a terrible reckoning with the state of affairs:

> My desperation lies in recognizing the bitter facts. For basic things like my dance group, my school my dances, there is no real support. While for the big show everything is procured immediately … Victory of collectivism over the individual! … No living person can avoid it. One is involved in the big fabric. To try to tear it would bring self-destruction.

(ibid.)

Hedwig Müller concludes that Wigman did take note of the rising terrorism in daily life. But she did not elaborate in her diaries about the fear and the growing mistrust. Her focus remained on her work: the words "work" and "dance" and the events of her professional life dominate her diary entries and her correspondence. Reading them, one comes to realize that her dance life was her true existence. Every joy or trauma is chronicled primarily in relationship to her art. Müller also concludes that Wigman had become careful. And indeed it was true that one did not know how concealed private life was. Müller writes that Hesschen guarded Wigman's privacy in the home. But ultimately she was a public person, by nature of her work. Wigman did attend a planning meeting in Munich on 6 May 1937. Upon her return to Dresden she wrote:

> Confused, broken, hit, smash. … What insanity. I still do not know what approaches me. I have to go into this hell … as the only woman among the men! Every objection, every doubt is pushed aside as tiresome and questionable.

(Wigman in Müller 1986a: 245)

In the end, Wigman stalled so long that the offer to choreograph for the museum dedication was officially withdrawn. The program went on without her. The day following Hitler's inauguration of the House of German Art, a very different exposition was opened across the street. Nazi exhibitions of *Entartete Kunst* or Degenerate Art made outcasts of the great modern German visual artists, including Wigman's old acquaintances from *Die Brücke*. Even long-time Party member Emile Nolde was ostracized as a degenerate artist in the 1937 cultural purge. Meanwhile, Wigman remained in Dresden, writing.

> Remain quiet – do not allow the nervous shivering to arise. Do not complain … nobody can take your rich life from you. Your creations may pass, you may be fast forgotten but maybe you have planted a few seeds and maybe the earth was fertile at some places.
>
> (Wigman in Müller 1986a: 250)

LEAVING DRESDEN

The once-fertile dancing ground of Dresden was becoming uninhabitable for Wigman. The city had maintained its reputation as a center for arts and culture during the first years of Nazi dictatorship, but all arts activities were increasingly governed from Berlin. Many cultural institutions began moving from the city of Dresden and Wigman also applied for such a move, to Berlin where Hanns Benkert was residing. In 1937, her application for relocation to Berlin was officially "unapproved" (Karina and Kant 2004: 272–3). There were more than 17,000 trials against Germans who opposed the regime in that year. Mary Wigman choreographed her *Autumnal Dances* in what appeared to be the fading light of her own greatness. Letters from officials reflect an effort to humble Wigman and to bring her into line with Party policy. She had lost her status. Yet she was remembered by some as a national treasure. Her diaries of 1938 reveal that she felt the opportunity for considering immigration had passed. "To go abroad? To the U.S.A.? It is not possible anymore" (ibid.). During that same year Martha Graham choreographed *American Document*, placing patriotism and optimism at the center of her work. While the American moderns were developing their own art, much in debt to Wigman and the German innovators, *Ausdruckstanz* was in decline.

On 9 and 10 November 1938, sanctioned violence against Germany's Jewish population was laid bare during the *Krystallnacht*, or the Night of Broken Glass. Jewish synagogues and property were brutally destroyed as officials relentlessly pursued a policy of Aryanization. By 1941, a police regulation required that all Jewish Germans wear the Star of David. The government placed a general ban on dance dramas and anything that did not comply with ballet traditions and National Socialist values. A specific ban of free dance or German expressive dance in public places applied to Wigman's work. But she did continue to perform in venues such as the Theatre Horst-Wesselplatz in Berlin. By 31 March 1940 she was presented in second billing to the students of dance theater there. She had become a political liability to Benkert after more than ten years as business and romantic partner. Traveling to Berlin in 1941 to teach a series of workshops, Wigman arrived at Benkert's house, suitcase in hand. Only then did she learn from Benkert's housekeeper that he had married a woman who was not only younger but who also had Party affiliations more advantageous to his own career.

Loss followed loss, yet Wigman revealed none of them in her extant letters to Hanya Holm in the United States. Only through her poems, letters, diary and her dances can we glimpse the depth of her bereavement, not only for the betrayal by Benkert but also mourning for her own willful allegiances to her nation and to her art. In 1942, the Wigman School, her home for decades, was sold to the city of Dresden. The Dance Academy that had been established within Wigman's school by Gretl Curth-Hasting, Gisela Sonntag and Hanns Hasting was subsumed into the municipal conservatory that ultimately absorbed the Wigman School. Another betrayal, this time by those with whom she had worked for years, added new bitterness to her losses:

As of today, this, my school, no longer exists. For 22 years, love, effort, care, also joy, beginning, center, expansion, good times, and bad times.

Now it is not only the name on the house that is disappearing; it is also the spirit that is departing.

(Diary entry: 2 April 1942)

Mary Wigman presented her final solo concert in 1942, essentially ending her performing career at age fifty-five. By September of 1942, the offensive at Stalingrad was under way and it proved the turning point of the war. In January the Wannsee Conference secretly laid plans for the "final solution," the systematic extermination of European Jewry. The Reich Propaganda Office further decreed the prohibition of abstract dance and symphonic music.

After 1942, government orders restrained Wigman from performing, but she was not left immobile. She was granted a position as guest teacher in Leipzig through her old friend Hanns Niedecken-Gebhard, who had supported her work as early as 1921 when he produced her *The Seven Dances of Life*. It appears that Goebbels did not want Wigman to hold a full-time position, but Niedecken-Gebhard could make accommodations on her behalf. As a well-positioned Nazi and head of the Department of Dramatic Art at the Music Academy in Leipzig, he was able to help Wigman work under tenuous circumstances, although she was never granted a full-time position there. Under a commission from Niedecken-Gebhard, Wigman worked with composer Carl Orff to stage *Carmina Burana* for a July 1943 performance at the Leipzig Opera House. In February 1944, Allied bombers destroyed the dance building at the Leipzig Music Academy, but Wigman continued to teach a handful of students in her apartment. Her diary reveals that she threw herself intensely into teaching until the declaration of total war in August 1944. At the end of the war, Wigman was left "physically and mentally isolated and exhausted, living under very deprived conditions in the East ..." (Partsch-Bergshon 1994: 116). A severe food shortage left Wigman suffering from malnutrition. Annie Hess had managed to keep some food on the table and, with care packages from Wigman's American students and friends, students continued to find refuge at her home. Wigman again opened a school in 1945 but, nearing sixty and in weakened physical condition, her hopes for survival lay in a new start in West Berlin.

TO BERLIN

In 1942, Wigman began a working relationship and friendship with composer Kurt Schwaen. Schwaen had been imprisoned from 1935 to 1938 as an enemy of the Nazi government, due to his membership in the German Communist Party. Released from prison between 1938 and 1942, he was conscripted in 1943 into the 999th Afrika Brigade, a unit made up of former political prisoners. Letters show that Wigman tried to counsel Schwaen in his unsuccessful efforts to avoid being drafted. Correspondence between Wigman and Schwaen shows her concern for his well-being, as well as her own unsettled position. On 5 November 1943, Wigman wrote to him:

The heart lies heavy with all that has taken place. Now many men whom I knew personally are suffering at Stalingrad. Also the new regulations lie like a heavy weight around my sphere of activity. Still, nobody knows what shape the occupation [by the Allies] eventually will take.

(Schwaen 2006: 14)

These letters starkly show how the focus of her attention, including how she perceived those in her life, revolved around her work and the belief that the work was larger than the chaotic times or the individuals involved. Schwaen was again losing his artistic life under the Nazis and despaired in his diary. He wrote that Wigman could in no way understand what such a conscription meant to him. But later he wrote that he had been wrong about her. Wigman took on Schwaen's wife as her accompanist, thus helping to support her while her husband was enlisted. And Wigman maintained her friendship with the Schwaens for many years.

Wigman continued to live and work in Leipzig under Russian occupation from 1945 to 1946. She directed the staging of Gluck's *Orpheus and Eurydice* at the Leipzig Opera in March 1947, using dancers from the opera house along with her student ensemble. She wrote: "On the surface, one goes on working as if everything was the same. Yesterday's technical rehearsal for *Orpheus* has shown me that the work – in spite of the defective material – could be good" (ibid.). In January 1946 Wigman wrote to Schwaen of the bitter cold in Leipzig.

I myself work in silence and must do this to be able to exist. I could have it differently if I could join in what one calls Agit-Prop under the KPD [the German Communist Party]. But I want no dependence that obliges or compromises me or lowers the level of my art. I'd rather fight for the penny than stoop to becoming a promotional symbol. I am still curious about the possibility of going to Berlin. Economically, things may prosper here again but culturally it seems dubious to me. Pity!

(Schwaen 2006: 19)

Later, in June 1949, Schwaen and his wife helped Wigman gain an invitation to relocate to the Wilmersdorf district of West Berlin. The magistrate of Wilmersdorf offered to support her school for one year, after which she was expected to take over financial responsibility. And international students were again coming to her, many from the United States. American dancer Bill Costanza recalls her all-encompassing grace and ability to communicate in many languages with the students who filled her summer courses. Other German colleagues who had lived through the war were aware of her early work and major contributions to the art form. But the students who populated her Berlin school were of a different generation. Growing up amid the chaos of war and coming of age in a defeated and divided Germany, shamed by the revelations of the Nuremburg trials, these young people felt a calling to their art very different from the calling Wigman had felt. While German dance was utterly disrupted by war, American modern dance had thrived. **Merce Cunningham**'s visit to Germany in 1960 was greeted with enthusiasm, his work hailed as the dance of the present.

Merce Cunningham (1919–) – dominant force in Modern dance since the 1960s. Graham company member from 1939 to 1945. Founded his own company in 1953. His fruitful collaboration with composer John Cage endured for fifty years.

And Mary Wigman was no longer performing. Brigitta Herrmann began her study with Wigman at the Berlin school in 1957 and continued a long association with Wigman until she emigrated to Philadelphia in 1968. Herrmann said that when one was in the room with Wigman, she always left with the impression of a great artist. After Herrmann's early training in Russian ballet technique, which was the mainstay of the Palucca School, the possibilities of expressive dance at the Wigman School were a revelation. However, Wigman in her seventies could not be an active role model for the young dancers of the new Germany. Many of these students would not come to recognize the strength of her fundamental dance philosophy until later, if at all. And for others of the new generation, her poetic, emotive imagery seemed outdated. Just as the American postmodern dancers had turned away from the psychodrama of Martha Graham, young German dancers were looking for something new to inspire them. Dancer Helmut Gottschild said: "We were the first generation to come to consciousness after the war. The first generation to ask our parents how it could have happened. And suddenly we were confronted with Mary Wigman's pathos … " (Gottschild in Manning 1993: 227).

In many ways Wigman had become an outsider within the German nation to which she had dedicated her life and her art. She did continue to stage dance works during her final decades in Berlin. Working closely once again with an accompanist, Ulrich Kessler, she danced with her students in *Choric Studies II* in January 1953. Susan Manning interprets *Choric Studies II* as Wigman's coming to terms with her accommodation to National Socialism (ibid.: 235). Indeed, the intention of *Ausdruckstanz* was an ongoing mining of the depths of individual experience. In this, all her dances were autobiographical in the deepest sense. And the central role of the Prophetess was a natural one for Wigman. But in her diary, she describes her performance of the work as a sort of coming home, a returning to the stage and the transcendent moment when dance and life reach heightened vitality. Dore Hoyer, considered the most talented soloist of her generation, was to have danced the role initially but, when she cancelled, Wigman chose to step into the part. At the Berlin Wigman School it was Hoyer, not Wigman, who became the dancing model for students such as Brigitta Herrmann who were still drawn to the profound nature of *Ausdruckstanz*. And Hoyer was the soloist for Mary Wigman's last great choreographic effort on the concert stage, *The Rite of Spring* (1957). Once again, *Schicksal und Opfer* – Fate and Sacrifice – became the themes of Wigman's choreography as they had anchored the guiding philosophy of her life.

In the end, Mary Wigman allied herself with a music-driven theater that appeared far from the territory of her Absolute Dance. Still, she was able to use her talent to awaken dynamic space on the stage. Between 1954 and 1958 she set Handel's *Saul*, restaged Carl Orff's *Catulli Carmina/Carmina Burana* and Gluck's *Alkestis* for the National Theater in Mannheim. In 1958, she also made one last journey to the United States and met with Martha Graham and Ruth St. Denis, and it appears that the years of competition fell away in their meetings. In 1969, at age eighty-three, she visited Israel with life-long friend Herbert Binswanger, although most of her travel later in life was to Switzerland and the countryside that she had known and loved for so many years. Even though she became nearly blind, she could feel the landscape of those familiar mountains. In 1961, Wigman directed her final work. With Gustav Sellner, she choreographed Gluck's *Orpheus and Eurydice* in Berlin. Through this production her stage life came full circle. Nearly a half of a century had passed since those early, heady days of discovery at Hellerau, where her performing life began with the early study of *Orpheus* by Dalcroze and Adolph Appia. There seems no better myth than Orpheus with which to memorialize Wigman's life and career. The descent and return of Orpheus from Hades represented an ideology of metamorphosis and a metaphor for redemption. Wigman's dance became her own road to emancipation. Steeped in mysticism, Wigman's dance offered a sort of deliverance through ritualized practice and an aesthetic doctrine. As early as 1921, in *The Seven Dances of Life*, it is only through the dance that the character passes through death and attains liberation. The wedding of physical body and inner spirit defined Wigman's work to the end of her life. Mary Wigman continued to teach from 1961 to 1967, when she finally closed her studio. Suffering from failing eyesight and a weak heart, she died in Berlin during the fall of 1973. In April 1973 she wrote to Binswanger:

> Everywhere people are again surrounded by snow despite the fact that snowdrops and crocuses started to flower here too. I only know this from hearsay; for I am living in Hades, in the realm of the shadows, and there everything is in motion … it is rather like sinking and being lifted, swaying and tottering … I want to resign myself to it. I want to do what I can.
>
> (Wigman 1973: 200)

Even close to her death, her description remains rooted in her physical experience. She had made numerous dances in which she grappled with death. Even as she moved toward the end of her life she met her decline with a dancer's sensibility. When she was asked to write her biography in her final years, Wigman responded with a treatise on the dance art itself. She continued to make a case for dance as a profound art form. She broke open structures of movement invention and female objectification, only to be accused of performing madness on the concert stage. In the end she wrote:

> People like my dancing or they think it most terrible … It is hard for an artist to tell why her dance method is a success. I have tried to combine emotion with intellect. Some call my art tragic, far removed from sweetness and prettiness. I have tried only to interpret modern man and his fate.
>
> (Wigman 1973: 149)

MARY WIGMAN
„Hexentanz"

Verl. Hans Dursthoff, Berlin-W. 30.   1331.

Figure 7 Mary Wigman. Photographer unknown, courtesy of the Tanzarchiv Leipzig

2

MARY WIGMAN'S WRITINGS ON THE DANCE

A philosophy embodied

INTRODUCTION

Mary Wigman was a poetic writer. The drama that was inherent in her performance is reflected in her writing. And she wrote a considerable amount, revisiting and re-emphasizing what she felt was crucial to understanding the new dance. Wigman has appeared in and been the subject of many texts and articles. Studies dedicated to her life and work range from biography to general dance history, to critical theory. We can learn about Mary Wigman as an author through her primary writings available in English, which have been gathered in two volumes, both edited and translated by Walter Sorell: *The Language of Dance* (1966) and *The Mary Wigman Book: Her Writings* (1973). These are dominated by her emphatic belief in the important place of dance in culture. They also allow a glimpse into her unique thoughts on dance technique. Her life philosophy was singularly focused on the dance itself and her writings, while permeated with metaphysical references, are often surprisingly plainspoken as to the reality and demands of a life dedicated to dance. They remain relevant and compelling to contemporary performers. For this was her intention, not only to speak to her contemporaries, but also to develop an art that would take root and grow through time. Fortunately, many shorter articles by Wigman have been translated and are readily available to scholars and college and university students, if not on library shelves then electronically or through interlibrary loan. A video produced in 1991 by Allegra Fuller Snyder titled *Mary Wigman 1886–1973* contains film clips of Wigman speaking, dancing and teaching, making it a valuable resource. At the time of this writing, the German/French television channel *Arte* has aired a new biographical documentary on Mary Wigman that should make her story accessible to the general public in a new way.

THE LANGUAGE OF DANCE

Mary Wigman begins *The Language of Dance* by saying that her friends want her to write a biography. "What should I tell? My life? Life, fully lived is a rounded thing. It is better to let it be and to let it complete its course instead of cutting it into small pieces like a birthday cake" (Wigman 1966: 7). Instead of recounting her own story from birth to old age, Wigman charts a different course.

> To live life and to affirm it in the creative act, to elevate and glorify it? That is what I want to write about ... for all of you who love the dance ... the result is not going to be a textbook. Nevertheless it may have something to say to you and may help you to come closer to the meaning of the dance. Its secret? That lies hidden in the living breath which is the secret of life.
>
> (ibid.: 8–9)

Rather than a systematic study, *The Language of Dance* presents the beliefs and values that shaped Mary Wigman's dance life. She is also compelled to give suggestions for the working dancer. Her intentions are twofold: first, she wishes to speak to the dancers of the future, to encourage their enthusiasm for the art through her own passionate ideals. Second, she chronicles fifteen of her dances, from her 1927 *Ceremonial Figure* through *Farewell and Thanksgiving* from 1942. Here she attempts to lay bare her choreographic intention, her emotional responses and inspirations for these dances.

In the introduction to *The Language of Dance*, she proposes the concepts of time, strength and space as the elemental vocabulary from which dance is developed as a language. And she makes a case for their recognition as the primary elements that give dance vitality and variety of expression. The key to her philosophy is found in the very name *Ausdruckstanz* – dance meant to express, dance as embodied language.

The dance is a living language that speaks of man – an artistic message soaring above the ground of reality in order to speak, on a higher level, in images and allegories of man's innermost emotions and need for communication.

(Wigman 1966: 10)

There is no question that for Wigman the drive to dance came from an overwhelming urge to communicate. However, this need grew not only from the longing to have her feelings heard but also more from a sense of obligation to experience and thus share the fully lived moment. In these moments, the human condition could be elevated from daily existence to the realm of the metaphysical. She felt her mission was to make this experience available to those watching. For Wigman, this mystical experience was the heart of the dance.

Wigman had said, "I do not believe in labels. One cannot take art and divide it into separate parts – this is Expressionism, this Modernism, this is Futurism, this is Post-Expressionism. There is expressionism in all art that is worthy of the name" (Wigman 1973: 149). Labels defining art movements sometimes dissolve or solidify over time as we attempt to categorize an artist's work. Like many Expressionist artists, Wigman meant to leave her mark on the world. Walter Sokel characterized the Expressionist as "an ethical idealist [whose] goal is spiritual, not material. It is the role of spirit on earth" (Sokel 1964: 146). This idea of the spirit was not linked to any organized religion but instead to a set of secular principles that might lift up humanity through individual effort. In an interview, Wigman said, "We have no uniform religion now to which to dedicate the dance. But in every person there is a deep religious sense that springs from a vision of the infinite. It deserves a common expression" (Wigman 1931: 42). Wigman recognized that awe and sacredness historically resided in dance and she attempted to imbue all her work with a similar reverence. And she was not alone. In the United States, Martha Graham had gone so far as to choreograph herself as God/dess in the role of the Virgin surrounded by dancing acolytes in *Primitive Mysteries* (1931). Graham dancer Gertrude Schurr said: "Everyone felt it, this belief in oneness. And when I was near her [Graham] she had the mystic verity of a figure to be worshiped" (De Mille 1991: 179). As early as 1917, Wigman presented a solo evening of "Ritual Performances" in which she performed her cycle of *Ecstatic Dances* including *The Nun* and *The*

Dervish. Why did Mary Wigman and her peers seek a new sort of reverent ritual practice beyond those available in churches? How had ideas of worship changed? And how did Wigman help to pioneer new ways of performative spirituality?

PHILOSOPHICAL CONTEXT

Charles Darwin's publication of the *Origin of the Species* in 1859 raised questions about the very source of life on earth. Untethered from religious moorings, the scientific mind seemed to light the new life path. And how was this life to be lived? What moral compass would point the way in this new world? In 1881, **Friedrich Nietzsche** began *Thus Spoke Zarathustra*. In that work, eventually published in 1887, and in the *Gay Science* (1882) he shocked the intellectual world with his declaration, "God is dead." Surely, Nietzsche did not murder God. He merely reported on the demise and speculated on who would receive the inheritance. Mary Wigman had been steeped in Nietzsche. She performed with the Dada artists at the Cabaret Voltaire while clutching a copy of *Zarathustra* and reciting from the book as she danced. The "Dancing Songs" of *Zarathustra* called for a new way of being in the world. In *Zarathustra*, Nietzsche expressed contempt for so-called "Despisers of the Body," who saw the physical body as something to be overcome for the salvation of the soul. In response Zarathustra claimed "the soul is only a word for something about the body" (Nietzsche 1966: 34). For Wigman, too, the sensuous dancing body became the vehicle to an authentic life. In her *Seven Dances of Life*, it is only through the power of her dancing that Wigman can be set free. Nietzsche's Zarathustra went on to say:

> If my virtue is a dancer's virtue and I have often jumped with both feet into golden-emerald delight ... all that is heavy and grave should become light; all that is body, dancer ... that is my alpha and omega: Oh, how should I not lust after eternity and ... the ring of recurrence?
>
> (Nietzsche 1966: 342–3)

Friedrich Nietzsche (1844–1900) – German philosopher and classical philologist who influenced most modern artists and thinkers. His texts include *The Birth of Tragedy out of the Spirit of Music*, in which he

Figure 8 *Totentanz der Mary Wigman*, Ernst Ludwig Kirchner, 1926/1928. Courtesy of the Tanzarchiv Leipzig

interpreted the relationship of man and world, life and mind as mediated by illusion, myth and religion. He laid out the modern argument for the interplay of the Dionysian and Apollonian aspects of human experience and in 1883 he wrote *Also Spoke Zarathustra* in which he declared there is no world beyond this one.

As we will see in Chapter 3, longing, love and lust are all performed as integral to the human condition in *The Seven Dances of Life*. And so is suffering. But through death there is rebirth and joy. But what are we to make of the dance of the demon that appears in this work? The theme certainly recurs throughout Wigman's creative life. Hedwig Müller sees this struggle with the demon as metaphor for Wigman's struggle with herself, the tussle between her innermost wishes and deepest fears. Modern use of the term "demon" leads us to assume an association with evil spirits and satanic figures. This relatively late semantic development evolved from medieval Christian ideas of good and evil. Wigman's use of the term hearkens back to older definitions. Initially, the Greek *daímōn* meant divine power, fate or god. In Greek myth, the *daímōn* of a hero could undergo a transformation and become as a god. Like the Roman term "genius," the term demon was originally used almost synonymously with "soul." For Wigman, such an enlarged sense of soul was what she sought through performance. This flew in the face of practicality and rationality. And these ideas certainly took Mary Wigman on a divergent path from her upbringing and social expectations. They also lent support to her driving ambition and simultaneously allowed her to claim that her inspiration stood on greater authority than her own ego. Such ambition, still considered unseemly in a woman, could be justified and elevated when coming from or demanded by a cosmic source. Understanding the *Zeitgeist* of her era is crucial when reaching back to grasp Wigman's values and philosophy.

Zeitgeist – literally the spirit or intellectual climate of the time.

Since the eighteenth century, the European Enlightenment had elevated science and reason over the irrational and the intuitive. Reason held the seat of authority. And in the larger society, a particular form of progress prevailed. The Romantic artists reacted with a nostalgic longing for an idyllic past that was deemed closer to nature and thus more authentic. These longings could not hold back the onslaught of the machine age, but traces of Romanticism remained in what we now call Modernism. Many early twentieth-century residents of Western Europe and the United States identified the human body as part of that more authentic, natural world that could be accessed through the *Körperkultur* or physical culture movement. Rather than denying physical existence, the body was seen as a tool for becoming a better individual and thus developing a better society. To facilitate building a healthier body, dance gymnastics came into popular culture along with bicycling, hiking, spa visits and other activities thought to build and sustain well-being.

In the midst of these developments, Wigman was hard at work attempting to redefine and claim a place for a deeper dance in the modern age. When Wigman danced and read to her audience *Zarathustra's* declaration that "the self is the body" and "reason lies in the body," she felt vindicated. The importance of harmony, between the individual and the group, shaman and community, mystic and acolyte, all seemed to be the oldest stomping grounds of dance ritual. And this ancient place for dance appeared threatened with extinction by the onslaught of science, technology, civility and respectability that had burst into the modern age under the banner of progress. In response to this upheaval, Wigman and the artistic intelligentsia turned to the philosophers to make sense of the modern world and redefine the manifest destiny of the artist.

Wigman was not the only aficionada of Nietzsche among the early modern dancers. The American pioneers Isadora Duncan, Martha Graham and Doris Humphrey all referred to Nietzsche as a key influence on their work. Why was Nietzsche so compelling for them? According to Nietzsche, the act of creation was bequeathed to the artist by a dying God. If God is dead, man is empowered. After centuries in the service of faith, the creative urge became the key to fulfillment and a measure of individual greatness, and thus the realized potential of humankind. And there was a place for women in this new pantheon. For Wigman and other modern dancers, the concept of the artist as *Uberfrau* was contagious, deeply compelling and validating. When God dies, humans can be as gods and the artist can become the godliest of all. Never before had the vocation of art held such power, especially for the female artist. She dressed sensuality in the trappings of mysticism and a connection with a higher, and not necessarily patriarchal, life source.

Early twentieth-century Germany produced many artistic thinkers who shared Wigman's beliefs. She was in no way an isolated figure. In their world-view, social change could be effected through the practice of art. Through her excavations of meaning in dance, Wigman bears a resemblance to another Expressionist, the painter Wassily Kandinsky. She shares his belief that spiritual impulses could be made visible in art. In fact, for Kandinsky, Wigman and many Expressionists, the acts of making art and viewing art should generate higher human consciousness. Further, for Wigman at least, dance became the very experience of existence itself, or *Dasein*, a term that she shared with the philosopher **Martin Heidegger**. Nietzsche, Heidegger and Wigman all saw coming into *Dasein*, or a being coming into being, as the action of the most alive and fully aware individuals, wherein the divisions between body, soul and intellect disappear. The world of human possibilities now seemed limitless to these moderns. Convention, the status quo and staid respectability were ideas whose time had passed. Even the very meanings of words were being reconsidered. In *Being and Time*, Heidegger wrote: "Language is no longer the expression of a timeless web of meaning, but rooted in human activity" (Heidegger 1962: 165). For Mary Wigman, dance, by its visceral and sensate nature, was uniquely suited to the making of a new and fully realized language. Reading Wigman's writings, we are struck with her tireless efforts to explain the unspoken language of dance in literal terms. The urge to communicate that drove her dance art appears again and again in her writing.

Martin Heidegger (1889–1976) – German philosopher who studied phenomenology with Edmund Husserl. A prolific writer, his *Sein und Zeit* (*Being and Time*, 1927) was considered a most important work. In *Sein und Zeit*, Heidegger concentrated on the concept of *Dasein* as a particular kind of existence unique to humans. He argued that authentic life is possible if death is resolutely confronted and freedom exercised with a sense of its essentially creative nature. Heidegger displayed an enthusiasm for the Nazi regime early on and was rector of Freiburg University before resigning in 1934.

While Wigman's interviews, writings and lectures attest to fluency in French and English along with her native German, it was the language of the body that most compelled her. In many ways it was an entirely new dialect that she was inventing. Like other pioneers in the modern arts, she recognized all language as symbolic and all symbols as growing from the need to communicate. Many practitioners of the various art forms were taken by a pressing need to uncover the symbols intrinsic in their arts and make them fit the current world. In the drive for personal expression and immediacy, Wigman felt that she had to reject the codified dance language of ballet.

WHY A NEW DANCE?

> The ballet had reached such a state of perfection that it could be developed no further. Its forms had become so refined, so sublimated to the ideal of purity, that the artistic content was too often lost or obscured. The great "ballet dancer" was no longer a representative of a great inner emotion (like the musician or poet), but had become defined as a great virtuoso.
>
> (Wigman 1983b: 306)

Isadora Duncan had paved the way for a new form of dance at the end of the nineteenth century. And Diaghilev's *Ballets Russes* had proven that a radically new sort of ballet performance could be accepted in the young twentieth century. Beginning her life in dance at the age of 27, for Mary Wigman ballet training was never an option. Through her studies with Dalcroze and under the influence of Rudolph von Laban, Wigman had found models for movement innovation that could reveal the world as she knew it. She felt that ballet remained an artifact of another age. More importantly, she felt that ballet lacked the movement vocabulary to allow the contemporary dancer to connect her body to the larger world.

> The ballet-dancer developed an ideal of agility and lightness. He sought to conquer and annihilate gravitation. He banned the dark, the heavy, the earth-bound, not only because it conflicted with his ideal of supple, airy, graceful technique, but because it also conflicted with his pretty aesthetic principles. Times, however became bad. War had changed life. Revolution and suffering tended to destroy and shatter all the ideals of prettiness.
>
> (Wigman 1983b: 306–7)

As a member of a generation of young people who had chosen to turn away from the circumscribed lives of their parents, Wigman sought a way to make meaning out of a world very different from that of her childhood. By the time she was ready to embark on her independent dance career in 1919, she had seen the Western world torn apart in a devastating war of attrition that had been called the "war to end all wars." In her writing, the territory of ballet could only represent an obsolete world. In this she is a quintessential modern artist. That she used the human body, and a female body at that, locates her among the great artistic innovators of her time and place. How can we place her in the context of radical modernism?

TWO STREAMS OF MODERNISM

In the task of defining modern Western sensibility and Mary Wigman's place in her milieu, two streams of thought pour from the earlier wellspring of the Renaissance. Both streams have deep sources in classical humanism and exhibit an optimistic estimate of human potential. And both streams reflect a general rebellion against authoritarian traditions: Church, feudalism and monarchy. Concerned with the events of this world rather than the afterlife, both reflect a belief in individual human genius or, at the extremes, a call for a cult of the hero. Put most simply, these two streams have come to be known as the Enlightenment and the Romantic response.

Was Mary Wigman an Enlightenment thinker or a Romantic? For the Enlightenment *philosophes*, hope for a solution to the problems of humankind lay in reason, not superstition or the authority of unexamined religious tradition. Reason applied to the evidence of the senses and scientific experimentation would drive modern civilization forward. Values were no longer solely tethered to religious morals. The future appeared full of possibilities awaiting the minds of Newton, Benjamin Franklin and their empirical heirs. The Enlightenment fueled the American and French revolutions by replacing the "divine right to rule" of the European monarchies with the concept of universal human rights.

Enlightenment thinking also kindled a Romantic response. While the Enlightenment mind saw nature as a locus for scientific experimentation and the source of raw materials that would drive industrialization, the Romantics made nature into the container of spirit and a place of mysticism, mystery and revelation. This was an idealized nature that could replace an authoritarian Godhead as source of life and moral compass. And nature and the female were often linked in Romantic literature, painting and dance. For the Romantic, inspiration, imagination, spontaneity and passion were nourished by the natural world wherein individual genius could flower. In contrast to Enlightenment optimism, the Romantics questioned progress and called for mankind to live more authentically through communion with nature and contact with other cultures supposedly untainted by civilization. Certainly, Wigman's experiences at Monte Verità and her subsequent choreography place her beliefs firmly within Romantic philosophy and aesthetics.

However, both streams of modern thought were fueled by essential breaks in perceptions of the human place in the world. These narcissistic injuries, to use the clinical psychological term, can generally be linked to three shifts in modern subjectivity. The first break had occurred earlier, with the Copernican/Galilean rejection of the Earth's fixed place at the center of things. No longer did the universe revolve around us. We were revolving around the sun. Aristotelian and ecumenical teachings, along with creation myths, were set trembling, prompting the Church to seek a new stasis through strict adherence to dogma and political control by the crowns of Europe. This new ordering seemed to be working, until the liberal breakthroughs of the US and French revolutions. The second narcissistic crisis came with Darwin's writing. While ideas of natural selection had been circulating in the scientific world long before Darwin sailed on *The Beagle*, the confrontation with his findings served as the point of rupture between the rational modern mind and old belief systems. Creation myths were relegated to antiquity, and Wigman was hard pressed to return myth and ritual to the modern dance world. Finally, a third break came with Freud's theories, as rational man discovered he was not even in complete possession of his own mind and that unconscious forces shaped his very behavior. Wigman was closely bound to practicing psychoanalysts in the formative years of her career. Although linked to practitioners of phenomenology and Freudian ego theory, hers was ultimately the inherent narcissistic struggle of the performer as artistic subject.

What did these shifts mean for the modern artist in the first decades of the twentieth century, and specifically for Mary Wigman? She and her fellow utopians sought the very wellsprings of human metamorphosis while craving more genuine practice of art. These ideas bound Wigman to dance and to dance absolutely. She and many other modern dancers had chosen to forego those creative acts that historically had remained entirely in the woman's realm: traditional marriage, childbearing or childrearing. Wigman saw that her role was to redefine and claim a place for dance in the modern age. She felt she could return dance to a place of power, far beyond mere entertainment.

Wigman's world-view serves as a prism through which we can glimpse the artists of her age. Culture and era shape the way the body moves. Dance, as the enduring vehicle of ritual, has reflected the acknowledged or submerged myths of culture and thus shaped the very movements that embody the myth. In Wigman's time this primal role of dance not only endured but also re-emerged to fill a new century. She had been born in the nineteenth century and that century had introduced the lightness of the French Romantics through the *ballets blancs*. In *La Sylphide* (1832) women hover as virginal figures literally suspended above the ground with wings on their backs, balanced on the tips of their toes. While Théodore Rousseau and the French painters went to the forest of Fontainebleau to create new landscapes, the choreographers Taglioni and Perrot drew on the librettos of Théophile Gautier and Novalis, and choreographed idea-lized women as unearthly sylphs to inhabit those Romantic landscapes. Wigman and her cohorts rejected both these dance predecessors and the hierarchical constraints of the Imperial Russian classical ballet. They emphatically broke open the moving body, just as the cubist painters fragmented the depicted figure. Even Isadora Duncan had sought to dance the lost glories of Greece with flowing feminine gestures, to the lush accompaniment of the great composers. Mary Wigman would strip all of this away.

PRIMITIVELY MODERN

Just as the Expressionists began to dominate German painting, Wigman's *Ausdruckstanz* became wildly popular in the midst of the political revolution, economic depression and social upheaval that devastated Germany after the First World War. Participation in gymnastics, movement choirs and *Ausdruckstanz* became a pop-culture craze for the war-weary citizens of the Weimar Republic who hungered for a life-

Figure 9 Emil Nolde, *Tänzerinnen*, c. 1912. Courtesy of the Tanzarchiv Leipzig

affirming physical culture. And this quest for physical experience was evident not only in Germany but also in the health and new life movements in the United States, where the wheels of industry turned ever faster.

The advent of the machine age is paradoxical at its core: just as some viewed such progress as an evil that destroyed true humanity, others appreciated their ever-expanding world-view. As transportation became more rapid and available, people were able to see images and artworks from faraway places. As the cities grew, swelled by laborers leaving their rural roots, the greater world contracted with the importing of art and artifacts to the museums of Europe. Rarely seen before, these images were startling and inspirational. In the early 1900s, museums such as the Anthropological-Ethnographic Museum in Dresden displayed what was termed "primitive" art collected from Africa, Asia and the South Seas. Among the artists, these works were hailed as artifacts from cultures where life was somehow more original and untainted by the modern world. The influence of African sculpture on Picasso's early work is well known. Specifically, a series of photographic postcards from Senegal provided him with a new source of posture, gestures, costumes and faces that were crucial to his groundbreaking work of 1906–7. By the 1920s, Mary Wigman would add Japanese Noh Theatre masking to her dance. Wigman's friend the painter Emil Nolde was attracted to these exotic art pieces and the people who created them. In 1914 he wrote:

> We live in an age where whole wilderness regions and primitive peoples are being ruined. Not even one small piece of primitive wilderness with its native inhabitants will remain. These primitive people within their natural surroundings are one with it and a part of the great unity of being. At times, I have the feeling that they are the only real humans, that we are some sort of over-educated mannequins, artificial and filled with dark longings.
>
> (Bradley 1986: 82)

Many of the Expressionist artists, including Wigman, tried to recapture the perceived immediacy and visceral quality of this art in what came to be called Primitivism. Primitivism as a concept grew from the anthropological idea that some cultures should be classified as complex and some as primitive. In fact, it was the study by European and American anthropologists of cultures unfamiliar to them. They proposed that these people descended from unchanged earlier cultures and therefore considered them primal. They also saw these cultures as endangered, soon to be rendered impotent by the forces of modernist expansion.

These artists, and particularly the dance artists, felt the idea of Primitivism was relevant, holding the promise of the return of art to a prime or first place within society. Indeed, many of these artists genuinely assumed a greater kinship to artists of all cultures than to bankers or merchants in their home territory. Mary Wigman attempted to redefine and claim a new place for dance in the modern age, even as the oldest sources of dance ritual had been threatened with extinction by the onslaught of technology and the relegation of dance to entertainment. In 1927, D.H. Lawrence wrote *Mornings in Mexico*, in which he continued to champion the idea that modern man must bring instincts and emotions into balance with intellect. Lawrence passed through Monte Verità and in many ways become the most eloquent recorder of the motivations and desires of his fellow artists, Wigman included. Lawrence made theatricality and authenticity tenets of his critique of contemporary life. He compared the relationship between the audience and the action onstage as a reflection of the distancing of modern man from authentic life:

> We go to the theater to be entertained … We want to be taken out of ourselves … We want to become spectators in our own show … Which is very entertaining. The secret of it all, is that we detach ourselves from the painful and always solid trammels of actual existence, and become creatures of memory …

> (Lawrence 1927: 97–8)

Embedded in Lawrence's prose is an argument for a turn toward a particular way of "becoming" or what Wigman would term *Dasein*. This is precisely what she would claim as the dancer's task in the world: a physical "being present" that seemed to have passed away in contemporary life. Wigman also took to romanticizing the American Southwest during her 1932 tour. Both Wigman and Lawrence felt that the dance lends itself more to this sort of becoming than does any other art. In her travels across the United States, Mary Wigman had been taken by the expansive landscapes and native dancers of the Southwest. After viewing the pueblo dances in Taos, New Mexico, Lawrence wrote:

> … perhaps they are giving themselves again to the pulsing, incalculable fall of the blood, which forever seeks to fall to the centre of the earth, while the heart, like a planet pulsating in an orbit, keeps up the strange, lonely circulating of the separate human existence … There is none of the hardness of representation. They are not representing something, not even playing. *It is a soft, subtle, being something.*

> (ibid. 106–7, 110)

KINESTHESIA AND KINETIC EMPATHY

For today's dancer, Wigman's quest remains crucial: how can bodily movement alone serve as a language with which to communicate an immediate experience of being in the modern world? How can dance allow the artist to truly be present in this world? While the questions appear metaphysical, they are grounded in physiology – muscle and bone. Two interrelated ideas arise in response to these questions. The first is the physical process of kinesthesia, which is the awareness of the position and movements of parts of the body by means of the proprioceptors or sensory nerves within the muscles and joints. We use kinesthesia all the time to know whether we are upright or upside down, to step off a curb safely or to get food from plate to mouth. Kinesthesia is a kind of muscular perception that allows us to consciously identify and thus direct our movements, certainly a crucial faculty for a dancer! A second concept, kinetic empathy, resides alongside kinesthesia in the language of dance. It is no wonder that Wigman dedicated her life to deciphering this language. To truly use dance as language, the message of muscle, joint and bone must travel beyond the dancing body to communicate with those watching. Setting aside the specialized and codified vocabulary of ballet, Wigman embarked on a search for new forms of gesture and movement that could be experienced more fully by dancer and audience alike. What she was mining was a sort of kinetic empathy, with roots closer to ritual and communal dance than to concert forms established at that time. Critic John Martin used the term "metakinesis" to describe this particular approach to the dance experience.

> Movement, then, in and of itself is a medium for the transference of an aesthetic and emotional concept from the consciousness of one individual to that of another … we see in the dance the relation that exists between physical movement and mental – or psychical, if you will – intention.
>
> (Martin 1933a: 14–15).

In Wigman's version of kinetic empathy, the dancer places herself so deeply into the dance expression that the tensions and motor responses of the dancing body are made visible and thus transmitted by means of a visual-kinetic communication – from bone to bone, muscle to muscle and cell to cell – to those watching. We use kinetic empathy daily to read the moods of others through their facial expressions, gestures, gait and posture. We simply refer to this as body language. The expressions to "feel it in your gut" or to "lighten up" are just two common examples of spoken language derived from physical communication. The challenge lies in transposing such non-verbal communication to the heightened physicality of the dance. John Martin wrote:

> When we see a human body moving, we see movement which is potentially producible by any human body and therefore by our own; through kinesthetic sympathy we actually reproduce it vicariously in our present muscular experience and awaken such [emotional associations].
>
> (Martin 1936: 110)

The applause that exploded in response to Nijinsky's leaps, the suspension of Pavlova's arabesque, and the thirty-two *fouettes* in *Swan Lake* burst spontaneously from the spectator's thrill and startled appreciation of virtuosity. These physical feats are heroic humanity made visible through the human body. And each observer recognized his possession of a body made in the same image. In that moment the audience can become unified through the kinetic experience: to each other and to the performer.

Mary Wigman chose to dig deeply into her personal experience to find new ways of moving that could convey the range of human conditions in such a direct and visceral way. This was her gift. Her stated goal was to go beyond the merely personal to universal human understanding.

> The primary concern of the creative dancer should be that his audience not think of the dance objectively, or look at it from an aloof and intellectual point of view, – in other words, separate itself from the very life of the dancer's experiences; – the audience should allow the dance to affect it emotionally and without reserve.
>
> (Wigman 1983b: 306)

In her abstract dances, Wigman did not intend to dance a message that could be translated into a specific outcome or text. Rather she trusted that each member of the audience would bring to the work their own meanings in the same way that we can hear multiple definitions and meanings in vocabulary or learn things from words that are not consciously intended by the speaker. In the experience of dancing, performing or watching, there appeared to be room for many interpretations.

> If my dance awakes a reaction, an experience, a pleasure, visual or emotional, it is satisfactory. A woman once said to me, "Do you know, when you were executing your dervish movements I understood the dance. You were a witch picking daisies in a field. I actually saw the daisies. That was it, wasn't it?" Now what could I say to this woman? If she thought I was picking daisies, well, all right. But I thought I was dancing.

> (Wigman 1973: 145–6)

While she did not always intend to put forward a dance narrative, a danced story that could be read consistently, Mary Wigman did want to create an intensity of experience. Her own body became her laboratory. How did she shape her body into an articulate vessel that could form a new vocabulary and generate kinetic empathy? For the foundation of this training she built on Laban's ideas of effort or force in the moving body. And beyond these, she developed a performer's understanding of muscular tension and release.

SPANNUNG AND *ENTSPANNUNG*

When John Martin visited Germany for the Third Dancer's Congress, he reported in the New York Times:

> Grope as one may through the many studios busy with pupils … performing their strenuous gymnastics or beating on their rackfuls of gongs and drums … watching carefully the strange intensity of body and mind that by a sort of kinetic sympathy wearies the watcher perhaps more than the dancer; … [and] learn as one soon must, to bow the head with at least a feigned reverence at every mention of those mystic words "Entspannung" and "Abspannung."
>
> (Martin 1930: *New York Times*, 3 August, 101)

The early explorers of dance modernism went into the studio to rediscover the deepest drives of the dancing body. Duncan had located the wellspring of movement in the thoracic cavity, the solar plexus. Martha Graham seated the source lower in the pelvis and accessed it through the contraction and release. Doris Humphrey identified the fall and recovery as the metaphoric "arc between two deaths." When Wigman wrote that the secret of the dance "lies in the living breath," she was describing what Duncan, Graham and Humphrey had all found: the expansion of the in-breath and the condensing of expiration was a physical truth that could be carried beyond the container of the lungs.

Wigman's concepts of *Spannung* (tension) and *Entspannung* (release) encompassed all of these sources for initiating movement. For Wigman *Spannung* and *Entspannung* were principles that allowed for a continuum of energy that either increased or decreased in effort depending on what was being expressed. Imagine placing your body in extreme tension, as though you were pushing with all of your strength against a solid, unyielding wall. Try it with a solid wall. The reaction of your muscles and joints is specific to that forceful effort. In contrast, envision yourself relaxing and reclining on a warm, sandy beach while the fingers, hand and arm move through the balmy air above, catching the breeze. These ways of moving create very different messages for those watching, and Mary Wigman used these very images to choreograph her *Hexentanz* in 1926 and her *Pastoral* from the 1929 *Shifting Landscape* dance cycle. While these are examples of the opposite poles of tension and release, the whole idea was big enough to allow for many subtle gradations of muscular effort between the two extremes.

The terms *anspannen* (to tighten or stretch the muscles), and *abspannen* (to loosen or relax them), describe the ebb and flow of muscular impulse. Sharp and bound or smooth and flowing, such muscular tension affects the overall shape and message of the moving body. Rather than execute a traditional step like a *jeté* or a *pirouette*, Wigman felt that movement and gestures derived from such variation of muscular tensions were the real vocabulary of the body and the language to which those watching would respond. Choreographers, critics, teachers and dancers now use the term "dynamics" to express these fundamental dance qualities. The term has a rich source in Wigman, who viewed her dance as a reflection of life and the struggle of the individual within the world. Larger forces always were at play in her choreography: the confrontation between the human and the cosmic. For her dance was true dynamism: the action of powerful, unseen stresses and influences, made visible.

SPACE

Spannung and *Entspannung* can shape the dancing body, but to what outside pressures is this body reacting? While her inner emotional landscape provided her dance motivation, Wigman was equally enlivening and responding to the physical space around her. Hanya Holm said: "In the realm of space particularly, I feel that Mary Wigman has made a great contribution ... In her dances she alternately grapples with space as an opponent and caresses it as though it were a living sentient thing" (Holm in Wigman 1973: 161). Conscious use of space has long been recognized as a hallmark of *Ausdruckstanz*, but of course dance by its very nature exists in time and space.

How was Wigman's use of space revolutionary? For Wigman the space became alive with a tangible substance of its own that could make greater metaphysical pressures visible through the dancing body. Martha Graham's mentor **Louis Horst** had tried to define Wigman's preoccupation with space: "Mary Wigman conceived of space as a factor like time, with which to compose" (Soares 1992: 18). He proposed that Graham and other American dancers "did not feel the enmity of limiting space" (ibid.). Horst was astute in observing that the contested borders of Germany sharply contrasted with the expanse of the American plains to which Graham gave homage. But another, complementary factor deserves consideration. Space for Wigman was not simply a location in which to dance but it became her great, invisible partner. In her solos, just as Duncan had proclaimed before her, Mary Wigman never danced alone.

Louis Horst (1884–1964) – pianist, composer and theorist, Horst was the musical director for Ruth St. Denis and Martha Graham. He exerted a huge influence on the emerging modern dance and on Graham in particular. In 1934 he founded the journal *Dance Observer* and in 1937 published *Pre-classical Dance Forms*, which was required reading for many early students of the dance.

Wigman had been introduced to new ideas about space during her time with Rudolf von Laban. Laban would go on to evolve his theories of pedagogy and Wigman would take a performer's route, developing a relationship to space that was more sensual and immediate. Her relationship with the space was intimate, tactile and thus able to inform the body as to levels of tension and release. She could literally feel the space against her skin.

> There she stands, in the center of space, eyes closed, feeling how the air presses down upon her limbs. One arm is raised, timidly groping, cutting through the invisible space, thrusting forward, with the feet to follow: direction established. Then, as if the space wanted to reach for her, it pushes her backward on a newly created path: counter-direction: a play of up and down, of backward and forward, a meeting with herself, battling for space within space: DANCE. Soft and gentle, vehement and wild.
>
> (Wigman 1973: 121)

For Wigman, the space around the dancer became the metaphor for the cosmos. Hanya Holm explained that the entire orientation of Wigman's dance was toward the establishment of a psychological and emotional relationship between the individual dancer as representative of humankind and the surrounding world, whether that world was seen or unseen. Wigman was continuously reacting to perceived forces in the universe and being moved by these universal forces. This philosophy was the foundation for the emotional, spatial and functional aspects of all of Wigman's work, whether in performance, in her choreography or in her teaching.

TIME, MUSIC, RHYTHM

Space, time and strength or effort, those fundamental building blocks that Wigman had outlined in *The Language of Dance*, were also continuously addressed in her work. The space informed her dancing body and how that body used *Spannung* and *Entspannung*. Sharp or smooth, percussive or sustained, such muscular tension affects not only the shape of movement but also the time in which the movement is performed. For Wigman, rhythm was established by the body rather than coming from an external or pre-created music source.

> It is the rhythm of the dance, which releases and engenders the musical rhythm. The musical accompaniment ought to arise from the dance composition. Of course, any music thus created can never claim to be an independent

work of art. The profound union formed in this way between dance and music leads for both to a total entity.

(Wigman 1973: 122)

Without the outer impulse of music, Wigman turned inward in her quest to generate movement in the subjective state. She sought an individual and psychological source of dance, closer to trance state than to technical brilliance or lyric musicality. However, Wigman did not see this as a simple regression or a turning away from dance conventions. Her desire was to make an original kind of dance ritual for a new age.

It should not be a matter of wonderment or confusion to say that our technical age engendered the dance-motivated being. When we now consider that the primitive force or rhythm is behind the motor; that every machine breathes and symbolizes harnessed rhythmic force, and at the same time, when we recall that the impetus of the dance is also rhythm, we then have a definite foundation, a common nexus between the seemingly opposed expressions of life and forms of art.

(Wigman 1983b: 306)

Photos of Mary Wigman in her school reveal much of the studio space dedicated to an assortment of instruments: gongs and whistles, drums and other percussion instruments and a piano. Wigman's students all learned to accompany the dance. And in its relationship to music, dance remained the leader. Since her time with Dalcroze, Wigman had sought to move the place of dance to the forefront, no longer dependant on music. Although Nijinsky and Duncan earlier had rejected the codified vocabulary and narrative conventions of ballet, Wigman went farther, detaching herself from the reliance on music that remained in Nijinsky's choreography of *Rite of Spring* or in Duncan's many solos. Along with her revolutionary ideas about space, Wigman also aimed to help free the dance from its subordination to music, especially after receiving support for this impulse from von Laban. She had worked with several of the great European orchestras and in her later years she would undertake major projects set to the music of Carl Orff and Igor Stravinsky. Writing in 1931, she allowed that, while music often evoked a dance reaction in her, when she developed the theme of a dance she consciously parted company with music. Instead of following a set musical score, she chose to work collaboratively with her musicians so that sound and movement would develop together. She sometimes danced in silence and at times incorporated the spoken word, as in *Totenmal* and *The Seven Dances of Life*, but always the accompanists were to support or enhance the movement rather than to lead it.

This way of working presents a very different experience for the performer. The performer is ultimately in control of the timing of the dance and each performance can thus be a revelation to the dancer. For Wigman, this was in keeping with her belief that the goal of performance is transcendence. Rather than following a set tempo, the solo dancer is free to fulfill the movement as the moment demands. Today, it is not surprising to find music as secondary to dance performance or added by such chance practices as those developed by Merce Cunningham and John Cage. Wigman was the first to introduce these ideas to performance, radically changing the relationship between movement and music in concert dance. This remains another of her major contributions to the modern dance.

THE MARY WIGMAN BOOK

Mary Wigman's radical innovations in dance performance also presented a new way to approach dance composition. She called for an original way of training the body. While she shied away from making a "textbook" for dance, she wrote about the things that she felt were fundamental to the new dance in the modern world. In 1933, Wigman contributed sections describing the foundations of her teaching methodology in Rudolf Bach's *Das Mary Wigman-Werk* (*The Work of Mary Wigman*). Much of her writing for Bach was later translated in *The Mary Wigman Book*. In the 1960s Wigman began to write her memoirs, beginning with reminiscences of her time at Monte Verità and the early years of her career as an independent artist. She continued through the establishment of her schools with stories of her students, many of whom became major figures in the history of the art.

The second section of *The Mary Wigman Book* is entitled "Statements on the Dance," in which are gathered many of her essays from the 1920s and 1930s. Wigman spoke directly to her methods of dance composition and offered ways to look at dance making that remain useful to contemporary dancers, choreographers and directors. In

1925 she was ready to put down what she had learned thus far in choreographing her own solo and group works. These became a brochure entitled *Composition* that was reprinted in *The Mary Wigman Book* (Wigman 1973: 85).

Wigman begins by admitting "There is no technique of composition," and that each dance work is unique in how it is made. As for compositional guidelines, she allows that each composition demands its own set of rules, which become manifest as the theme of each new dance is revealed in the choreographic process. Simply put, the rules for each particular dance develop as the dance grows. Thus, dance composition for Wigman is a creative process through which expression and function are joined. What does she mean by expression and function?

> Expression is the metamorphosis of subconscious, spiritual emotion into conscious, physical tangibility.
>
> Function is the power given us to use the body as an instrument for a visible portrayal of changes in our emotional moods.
>
> (Wigman 1973: 87)

The process that Wigman describes is twofold. First is an uncritical intuitive phase where the creative idea emerges from the inner consciousness and demands attention. We have already visited the basic tenet of *Ausdruckstanz* that demands the outward expression of inner emotion. And we have seen that Wigman's goal was to express conflicts and harmonies that arise with and between the individual and the world. In conceiving a dance she says, "The inspiration for a dance always arises from a heightened experience of life. ... It stirs in us a yearning, a stress, an urge to communicate" (Wigman 1973: 88). When Wigman writes that the "ability to compose is a talent. Talent is creative fantasy," she is referring to the ability to access these inner stirrings and bring them to the surface. This is an action of the imagination. In Bach's book, Wigman describes this part of composing as "not thinking" in which the idea comes to the choreographer as if in a dream, and in that form it may be carried for a long time before crystallizing into a theme. Thus improvisation was a key element of Wigman's training and teaching. In improvisation, the shifting nature and depth of internal feelings are accessed by moving the body. Wigman's sort of improvisation was deliberately structured to address particular questions about life experiences, formal concerns and inner states of being. As an example, she described returning from a restful vacation. With the joy of returning to the studio and meeting with her accompanists, she clapped her hands. Thus began the rhythmic and movement theme and a dance was born. But unleashing the feelings was only the initiation of the choreographic process. Wigman came to understand that even the most physically expressed emotion could only be the beginning of her dance composition.

Once the dance theme presents itself, the second part of the choreographic process begins. Through constructing and arranging movement sequences, the theme begins to take form. Everything that doesn't relate to the theme or that doesn't move the dance action forward is pared away so that the dance composition becomes clear in its simplicity. Thus the emotional content or expression prescribes the outward form of the dance. Ultimately, the chosen form then reveals the emotional content. At the beginning of her career, Mary Wigman had learned the importance of form in composition. In her early experiments with Laban, he despaired that her emoting was ruining his beautiful system. She grasped that expression must be carefully molded into a definite shape. She wrote: "I knew that, without killing the creative mood, I had to keep the balance between my emotional outburst and the merciless discipline of a super-personal control, thus submitting myself to the self imposing law of dance composition" (Wigman 1983a: 304). Clearly, her approach to composition and performance was drawing on much older ideas of bringing order to art.

WHAT DID WIGMAN MEAN BY ECSTASY AND FORM?

> Dance is the unification of expression and function,
> Illumined physicality and inspirited form.
> Without ecstasy no dance! Without form no dance!
> (Ohne Ekstase kein Tanz! Ohne Form kein Tanz!)
>
> (Wigman in Bach 1933: 19)

Wigman crystallized a multitude of ideas into that essential statement of her dance philosophy. The ancient Greek duality of ecstasy and form as interpreted by Nietzsche in *The Birth of Tragedy* found new life in

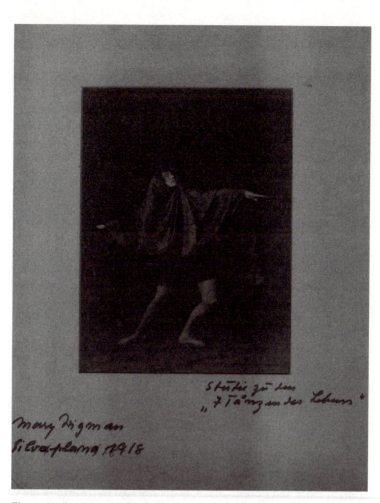

Figure 10 Early study for *The Seven Dances of Life*, Engadin, 1918. Photograph by Luise Schwabe, courtesy of the Tanzarchiv Berlin

Wigman's philosophy and in her performances. Though the term ecstasy has had many interpretations, the original Greek word *ekstasis* meant simply to stand outside oneself. The neo-Platonists considered ecstasy a divine gift of the gods that could lift mortals out of ordinary reality and into a higher world. They thought this transformative fire could burn away barriers between ourselves and our souls to illuminate our connection to the universe (Johnson 1987: vi). For Wigman, this definition of ecstasy would become the ultimate inspiration for dance composition and performance. When she declared, "Without ecstasy no dance!" she was claiming a place for her own art in an historic legacy. From her first dance experiences at Hellerau, she had been introduced to alternative, spiritual art practices that came to define her entire career. Drawing on the whirling practice of the dervishes that Laban had introduced to her, she created the *Drehentanz* (*Monotonie / Whirl Dance*, 1926) an embodied ecstatic practice, wherein she described the boundaries of her self falling away. Each time she entered the *Festspielhaus* at Hellerau, she passed under the large Taoist "yin–yang" symbol atop the entrance. The symbol of the dual distribution of forces, comprising the active or masculine principle and the passive or feminine principle, takes the form of a circle bisected by a sigmoid line. The two parts are invested with a dynamic relationship, with the one side representing the opposing and symbiotic force of the other. As the opposites exist with one another they engender perpetual motion, metamorphosis and continuity in the midst of contradiction. The surprisingly Eastern symbol in the center of a German planned community was meant to remind visitors and residents of the values upon which the community was founded and the shared cultural ideals of an integrated life based on rhythm, harmony, graciousness and simplicity. The yin–yang symbol that welcomed visitors to Hellerau was brought to the living, breathing body through much of Wigman's choreography and made manifest, specifically through her spinning practice. And this was ultimately a practice linked to older ideas of ecstatic experience.

If ever there was an iconic figure to represent Wigman's quest, it was the Greek god Dionysus. Dionysus had many names as the god of wine, abandon and madness. Thus, he represented the rebirth of life in the spring, the irrational wisdom of the senses and the soul's transcendence beyond the mundane. Those who chose to worship him were said to experience divine ecstasy. According to myth he was also initiated by the goddess Rhea into women's Earth mysteries. Thus, he represented the powers historically attributed to the feminine, though in male form. His worship was not confined to the temple ritual but grew into a sacred play that signaled the birth of western theater.

When she took the title "Priestess of the Dance" for her publicity materials, Mary Wigman was consciously linking her stage persona to a much older denomination. Historically, under Roman rule, Dionysus as Bacchus had been relegated to drunkenness and his strengths gradually became weaknesses. The loss of Dionysus was the triumph of rationality over irrationality and fact over intuition. In his place rose another powerful icon. Historically, Dionysus was not vanquished but set aside for Apollo, the god of order, reason and the light of the sun. Apollonian order esteemed facts and organized discovery, leading more than two millennia later to those markers of Enlightenment thinking: rational culture, science and progress. Though her impulses were Dionysian, Wigman knew that order must be imposed on her art for it to survive beyond her own ecstatic experience. When Wigman writes "Without form no dance!" she is referring to the external shaping, the choreographic laws that give a dance its outer form. Wigman knew that to become a professional dancer, she must tame her inner emotions into a tangible shape, a shape, however, that must retain its original link to the ethereal.

APOLLONIAN AND DIONYSIAN

Wigman recognized that her creative process required her to press the surging Dionysian vitality through conscious Apollonian crafting into form. This process proved irresistible to the Expressionists and, indeed, all of those modern artists who embraced their work with the passion of secular conversion. Wigman's own method of dance making embraced a kind of dialectic: the initial emotional content served as the thesis, the shaping of the form through conscious crafting served as antithesis and the synthesis was fused in performance when the emotion and form came together anew – equally transformed and transformative.

When starting a new work, she sought a subjective experience, releasing herself to a kinetic representation of emotion. She then gave shape to the raw material through objective, formal crafting. The final step was performance brilliance. Indeed, this quality made her extraordinary among the great dance artists and is one important reason for studying her performance philosophy. After giving the dance a set form, she attempted to synthesize both aspects of the creative process by returning to the original subjective emotional state in performance. In doing so she sought a transformative encounter for the dancer and the audience alike.

This is a demanding way to achieve performance success. She often stayed alone in the dark for long hours, seeking to come into the performance in a state receptive to metamorphosis. In so doing, she sought to create a transmutation between the dancer and the audience, what she called "the fire dancing between the two poles." The dance was a vessel built to hold the synthesized Dionysian and Apollonian experiences: the outer formal shape of the vessel held within its negative space the emotive heart of the dance. In order to accomplish such a restructuring of the artistic process, Wigman felt that she had to redefine the nature of dance itself. She saw herself as a defender of a new art that had brought total transformation and purpose to her life. To champion her art she had to break urgently from what she perceived as the stereotypical dancing girls that preceded her. She was a standard bearer for the new breed of dancing intelligentsia. Her themes were mystical and metaphysical, but her choreography was grounded in impeccable craftsmanship. While her writing delves extensively into the subjective and personal reasons to dance, she also methodically organized her process and formulated an objective approach to the craft of choreography. When trying to digest these elements that Wigman defined as essential ingredients of a dance, it is helpful to remember that her own early training was in music and that her time with Dalcroze was focused on studying music through movement. The elements that Wigman identified are all part of music composition and thus provide a window into the influences that helped shape her choreographic identity. Her use of these elements also ties her dance art to the larger world of art making and unites her efforts with contemporaries in many art forms and intellectual pursuits.

IDEAS ON COMPOSITION AND THE CHOREOGRAPHIC THEME

Wigman believed that, once a theme pushed its way into the choreographer's imagination, the dance was begun. By theme, she means a series of "small, related motions" which, when combined, constitute a dance movement that makes visible the underlying emotion (Wigman 1973: 88). The theme is essentially a map for exploration, and she called it the base upon which the composition rests. While the theme is born of the choreographer, it also takes on its own life and exerts its own rules, rules that she described as unique to each dance. So the theme must be big enough not to exhaust itself. And the choreo-grapher must be big enough to see the full range of creative possibilities in the theme. To this end, Wigman charted her seven essential ingredients of a dance.

1. First and foremost is the **main theme**, that series of movements that are developed in response to the dance concept.
2. Next comes the full **development of that theme** by exploring all of the theme's ingredients such as gesture, effort, time and space.
3. Once the theme is developed, **variations on the main theme** can take it into new directions using related developments.
4. The overall **structure or systematic arrangement** of the whole dance must be considered from beginning to end, and it must remain true to the theme and its movement ideas.
5. Wigman describes **dynamics** as kinetic start and stop, or a variation of the powers born of the dance. She further identifies dynamics as the rise and fall of dance tension. Thus the *Spannung* and *Entspannung* or tension and release experienced within the dancing body also is revealed in how the dynamics flow through the entire composition. Dynamics are "like a flame flickering through the dance form in direct proportion to its own intensity" (Wigman 1973: 89).
6. In addition to the dynamics of the whole, Wigman describes **nuance** as "color" or "lighting up" of a single phrase: placing an emphasis on a high point or moment of particular significance in the dance.
7. **Ornamentation** is harder to define. It calls up images of the quirky or surprising within a composition. Wigman calls it the embellishment of the main theme, making it more complex. It is a layering of theatrical and eccentric movement motifs on the original theme without obstructing its continuity. Wigman identified nuance and orna-mentation as the most idiosyncratic or revealing of the choreographer's personal preferences, allowing room for the dancer's unique per-formance strengths and style. In contrast, she says that structure and dynamics are more objective because they are ruled by the over-arching form of the dance as a whole (cf. Wigman 1973: 86–90).

Mary Wigman made a clear distinction between what she called com-position of design and pure composition. Composition of design has pedagogical purposes. It is a dance etude and, like the musical etude, it is intended to develop a point of technique or to hone and display the performer's skill. Wigman saw the goal of this sort of composition as producing a particular technical dexterity. "It caters to the arrangement wherein the body acts as an instrument under the command of the mechanics of movement" (Wigman 1973: 90), and as such bears comparison with the movement studies and the swing scales that she explored with Rudolf von Laban.

In contrast to a composition or design, she saw a second kind of composition that she called pure, absolute dance composition that leads into "two great subdivisions of form" (Wigman 1973: 91):

1. The functional dances; and
2. The emotional dances.

She saw the functional dances as originating from "the sheer joy of exercise, from the pleasure of doing or acting." Thus, the function of these dances is to express the beauty and enjoyment of the body either by moving clearly through space as in the Minuet or the Sarabande or by playing with a prescribed musical structure as in the 3/4-time waltz. While not tied to such historic dance forms, they offer examples of formal themes that can be developed and restructured in a functional dance composition.

The emotional dances originate from another source. Wigman describes them as "those based on subconscious stimuli and spiritual agitation. They grow out of an inner stress, a compelling urge" (Wigman 1973: 90–2). Thus, the emotional dance grows from genuine human emotion embodied. When taken to performance, its goal was to provoke an emotional response in those watching.

WHO HAS INHERITED THE EMOTIVE DANCE LINEAGE OF MARY WIGMAN?

> I felt that I'd never seen dancing before. In this she has given us pure dance, without acting ... It made one feel so big inside. I wanted to cry. Somehow Mary Wigman's dancing does not make me feel that I am hopeless. In fact I feel that I can dance, that I have danced just like this!
>
> (Gentry in Newhall 2000: 34)

What Mary Wigman accomplished in performance was in equal parts simple and profoundly difficult. She laid bare her emotions in a sort of self-sacrifice to the dance and to the audience. She appeared at once strong and completely vulnerable and in so doing allowed those watching to come into contact with their own humanity and emotions. Not only was she a consummate artist, but also her reputation as a teacher was equally far reaching. Many, many students from Germany and beyond studied with Wigman over her years of teaching, through either a summer course or extensive training at her studio. It is difficult to fully gauge the impact of her influence. Young dancer Eve Gentry, who saw Wigman in San Francisco in 1932, went on to dance in Hanya Holm's original dance group from 1936 to 1942. Her admiration for Mary Wigman remained throughout her life. And she is only one example of Wigman's impact on the nascent American modern dance. As early as 1926, Louis Horst brought tales of Wigman's innovations from Europe to Martha Graham. And Graham and her cohorts came face to face with Wigman's art through her American tours in the early 1930s. John Martin wrote of Wigman as a source of pure inspiration and elucidation of the new dance. While the 1940s and 1950s kept her confined to Germany, Wigman continued to work with students as much as possible. Isa Partsch-Bergshon recalls Wigman working whole-heartedly with a handful of students under desperate wartime conditions in Leipzig. In 1963, students from the Wigman School, Katherine Inge Sehnert, Helmut Gottschild and Brigitta Herrmann established *Gruppe Motion Berlin*, which brought Wigman's lineage directly into the realm of contemporary dance. In 1968, Group Motion relocated to Philadelphia, and Wigman called Herrmann and Gottschild her children who traveled to the new world. Gottschild established his *Zero Moving Company* and taught for years at Temple University. He continues to choreograph and perform. With Manfred Fischbeck, Herrmann continues to teach workshops developed from the Wigman practice and has named her own American group *Ausdruckstanz Dance Theatre*. Wigman's former pupils have scattered across Europe and the United States, sowing the seeds of her dance ideas along the way. The German dancer **Suzanne Linke** had her early training in the Mary Wigman School and continues to carry on her tradition as a strong female soloist. The *Tanztheatre* of **Pina Bausch** is often referred to as an heir of Wigman's theatrical impulse, made more complex through contact with global and contemporary ideas of theater, technology and new views of what makes a *Gesamtkunstwerk*.

Tanztheatre – literally, dance theater, incorporating movement, text, props and sets.

Pina Bausch (b. 1940) – a student and past director of the Essen *Folkwang Schule*, where Kurt Jooss established the dance department in 1926 following Laban's ideas of *Tanz, Ton, Wort* (dance, sound, word). Bausch was a scholarship student at the American Juilliard School. She is the leading choreographer and developer of European *Tanztheatre*. Her company, *Tanztheater Wuppertal Pina Bausch*, regularly tours throughout the world.

The Japanese-born dance form of ***Butoh*** has deep roots in Wigman's teaching. And in *Butoh* we find the training goals and values of dance Expressionism living beyond Wigman's time. *Butoh* icon Kazuo Ono saw Harald Kreutzberg perform in 1934 and claimed that this performance was one of his earliest inspirations to dance. He studied with Wigman pupil Takaya Eguchi and continued that study following the Second World War. Japanese artists **Eiko and Koma** studied under Wigman assistant Manja Chmiel before they brought their own form of *Butoh* to the United States.

Butoh – an avant-garde dance form that originated in Japan in the late 1950s. The founders were Tatsumi Hijikata (1928–86), a student of the German *Neue Tanz* and Kazuo Ohno (b. 1906).

Eiko and Koma – in 1971 joined the Tatsumi Hijikata company in Tokyo and soon began working as independent artists in Tokyo. They studied with Kazuo Ohno, who, along with Hijikata, was the central figure in the Japanese avant-garde theatrical movement of the 1960s. They eschew traditional Japanese dance or theater forms, instead choreographing and performing only their own works. Their interest in the German modern dance movement and non-verbal theater took them to Hanover in 1972, where they studied with Manja Chmiel, who had

Ausdruckstanz, *Butoh* and *Tanztheatre* all were incubated in nations that had been great military powers and each dance form became prominent after those nations experienced stunning defeats in war. Wigman's *Ausdruckstanz* reached its zenith following the First World War. *Tanztheatre* came of age in post-Second World War Germany and *Butoh* directly followed the dropping of the atomic bomb on Hiroshima and Nagasaki. The searing reversal of fortune, humiliation, despair and reckoning with the most violent of human events all seem to have found a special vehicle in such dance expression. All germinated in a world of modern psychology and philosophical phenomenology with which Wigman certainly was well acquainted. Her friendships with Prinzhorn, Binswanger and others attest to her profound attraction to psychological thinking. Jungian psychologist Robert Johnson claims that the archetype of the Dionysian ecstatic had been suppressed by the very rationality that has made modern scientific progress possible, while Jungian Marie Louise von Franz cautions that an archetype such as the earthy Dionysus can only be confined for so long. "Our refusal to honor an ethical caring human drive [say, for ecstatic experience] can transform it [the drive] into something wild and destructive" (von Franz 1980: 4).

Critic **Walter Benjamin** is often quoted by those who underscore how aesthetics came to be used by fascist governments. In his essay, "The Work of Art in the Age of Mechanical Reproduction" Benjamin wrote, "The logical result of Fascism is the introduction of aesthetics into political life" (Benjamin 1968: 241). Benjamin hoped that advances in technology that he termed "mechanical reproduction" such as photography, film or sound recording would emancipate the work of art from its "parasitical dependence on ritual." He argued that the ritual roots of art served to entrance both the artist and the viewer, taking them toward dangerous irrationality (ibid.: 243)

Walter Benjamin (1892–1940) – Jewish-German writer and one of the most intriguing and original Marxist cultural theorists of the twentieth century. Driven from Germany in 1933 by the rise of Nazism, he settled in Paris. When the Nazis invaded France in 1940, he fled to the Spanish frontier, where, on being denied entry, he committed suicide.

In the second half of the twentieth century, historian George Mosse delved much more deeply into this "aesthetization of politics." Mosse discussed a sort of secular religion that grew up around the fascist festivals and rallies as a performance of Nazi ideology. Circumscribed separations between history and social criticism dissolve in the writings of both Benjamin and Mosse. Their works give voice to a critical rupture in thinking about art that necessarily arose after the shocking revelations of the Holocaust and the utter devastation of the Second World War. With the images of Nazi horrors and spectacles inextricably intertwined in the collective consciousness, it seems that we have embraced Benjamin's warnings against the "auratic" and have turned away from the irrational and ritual-driven art making. Choosing the cerebral over the visceral or diffusing emotion through abstraction and interruption have become hallmarks of postmodern art. Since the end of the Second World War and into the new millennium, much thinking about Mary Wigman has been teleological: seeing the war as an inevitable outcome and her work as nuanced as much by politics as by aesthetics. The danger in such thinking lies in compartmentalizing Wigman's life and art, losing sight of the woman while building an icon. It is much simpler to judge an icon than to empathize with Wigman's very human struggles and recognize our own biases and blind spots.

From today's vantage point, the indelible images of Nazi mass spectacle make us instinctively turn away from any mass movement and its potential to bind us together. Our contemporary perspective also raises suspicion of the mystical performance practices that Wigman espoused in her *Ausdruckstanz*. Studies of brain chemistry have proposed that the human being is "hardwired" for the unifying and transcendent experiences found in ritual, whether a rock concert or deep meditation. Anthropologist Ellen Dissanayake describes the public ritual of dance as "both a means and an end in expressing and reinforcing social cohesion" (Dissanayake 1988: 83). The human body in motion has served as breathing ledger upon which are recorded sweeping changes. Dancing bodies such as Mary Wigman's have choreographed the turning of art from religious observance to secular creation. While she was identified as the Priestess of the Dance, she was the practitioner of a particular devotion to the dance art. Her revolution was not just spiritual. In the twentieth century, it became at once a social and ultimately a political revolution. Historian William McNeill argues that the need for individual expression and communal movement is so essential to human nature that it forces its own return. Looking toward modern dance's second century, the question arises: Will dance retain its ritual purposes? Even as rituals transform to reflect a changing world, they continue to reveal and unify that world. These dual roles of building community by moving people together and making space for the professional dancer as shaman or priestess emerge again and again.

3

MARY WIGMAN AS CHOREOGRAPHER

Choosing the focus

It is a daunting task to choose which works of Mary Wigman best represent her aesthetic practice and philosophy. In order to do this we must consider a career that stretched from her first solo choreography in 1914 to her final production of Stravinsky's *Rite of Spring* in 1957. Over this span of forty-three years, Mary Wigman made more than 170 solo dances and nearly 80 group works. From intimate experience, she knew well that, "in ninety-nine out of a hundred cases the choreographer is author and director in one person" (Wigman 1966: 22). In *The Language of Dance*, she reflects on the inspiration, motivation and "back stories" that gave birth to fifteen of her dances, from the 1927 solo *Ceremonial Figure* to her *Farewell and Thanksgiving* (1942). And in the final chapters, Wigman reminisces about making *Totenmal*, which sparks thoughts on the group dance and the choric dance.

In most of her early works she was also the performer, both visualizing and crafting the work and serving as the vehicle for its realization. In this she was among the pioneering dance soloists who were also the creator-performers of their very individual works. Loie Fuller, Isadora Duncan, Ruth St. Denis, Martha Graham and Doris Humphrey all stand as examples of that unique era of the great choreographer-soloist. Certainly, such soloists came to make group works. As individual techniques developed and were codified, the idiosyncratic expression and charismatic stage persona of the soloist gave way to the unity and uniformity demanded by larger works.

Mary Wigman saw three distinct dance forms as representative of what she termed the "three great complexes of expression and form" of effective dance (Wigman 1966: 22). Of the three forms that she identified – the solo dance, the group dance and the choric dance – Wigman worked primarily in the realm of the solo and the group dance. The choric dance appears as an exceptional manifestation of the 1930s, not unique to Germany. The mid-1930s in the United States also saw experiments in choric or mass dance, carried westward by students who had studied the form in Europe and saw it as appropriate to American populist dance movements. Although Wigman's experience in the true choric form remained limited to her collaboration in the production of *Totenmal* in 1930, she was highly aware of the implications and demands of choric dance. It seems most useful to our inquiry to consider these distinct choreographic forms in choosing works that give a sense of the breadth of her practice. Thus, we will focus on the 1926 solo *Hexentanz*, the small group work *The Seven Dances of Life*, a brief consideration of the specific demands of the choric form as revealed by *Totenmal*, and a glimpse of two solos from her farewell concert in 1942.

SOLO AS SIGNATURE: *HEXENTANZ*

For each choreographer, one work can be seen as bearing a unique signature through time. This work should be done when the artist's technical and artistic identity has fully matured. It may not necessarily be the final work. In fact, most likely the choreographer will move onward to further develop artistic ideas and values and impart them to others. The "signature work" that I propose is one that comes from an embracing of self, the realization that one's singular human experience can be expressed in a dance that is thoughtfully and meticulously crafted because the ideas and beliefs embedded in the work have been waiting many years to take on a definitive form. Of course this also calls for a maturity that comes with experience and the self-confidence that comes with the acquisition of a set of skills that define a craft.

Hexentanz was such a dance for Wigman. Made in 1914, the original *Hexentanz* was the first dance she created while a student of Rudolf

Figure 11 Mary Wigman in *Hexentanz*, 1914. Photograph by Hugo Erfurth, courtesy of the Deutsche Tanzarchiv Köln

von Laban. What she described as her deepest "stirrings" were realized in dance form, opening the floodgates of artistic expression and pointing a clear direction toward what to do with her life. The social expectations of marriage and identity of *Hausfrau* were banished as she saw her role as dancer solidify. Later, she reminisced about her joy in the creation of the work, giving insight into its place in her development and her long relationship with the dance:

> After Laban had fully approved of the sketch for my first *Hexentanz* I was so overcome with joy that I jumped all over the studio, sprained my ankle, and could not move for a whole unhappy fortnight. But the witch dance was brought to life and continued to be very much alive. It became part of my first solo program. It had to undergo many changes and pass through many different stages of development until, twelve years later, it received its definite artistic form.
>
> (Wigman 1973: 36)

By the time she made the second version of the *Hexentanz* in 1926, Wigman had been operating her own school, had toured as a solo artist and established her own dance company. Through her teaching, she solidified her approach to dance technique while gaining confidence in her artistic identity through successful performances. This is when *Hexentanz* achieved its final form:

> I believe that *Witch Dance* was the only one among my solo dances which did not make me shake with stage fright before every performance. How I loved it, this growing into the excitement of its expressive world, how intensely I tried in each performance to feel myself back into the original creative condition of *Witch Dance* and to fulfill its stirring form by returning to the very point where it all began!
>
> (Wigman 1966: 42)

The 1926 version of the *Witch Dance* was conceived as the fourth part of a dance cycle she had begun in 1925 with three solos preceding it: *Ceremonial Figure*, *Veiled Figure* and *Ghost Figure*. Also in 1925, Wigman wrote her article on dance composition. Therein she identified what she called elemental dances as a distinct kind of emotional dance composition. Wigman defined these elemental dances as being the medium and symbol of those forces born of the soil. In her

Figure 12 Mary Wigman in the 1926 *Hexentanz*. Photograph by Charlotte Rudolph, courtesy of the Deutsche Tanzarchiv Köln

description of beginning the *Hexentanz*, she recalled being drawn again and again back down to "some kind of evil greed I felt in my hands which pressed themselves clawlike into the ground as if they had wanted to take root" (ibid.: 41). In *Ceremonial Figure*, she had begun to incorporate the mask into her performances, thus reintroducing the mask to the modern dance as a tool for metamorphosis. Long recognized as a means of transformation in ritual dance and ancient theater, Wigman reclaimed its sacramental and theatrical roots for the concert stage.

In her role as creator and performer of the *Hexentanz*, Wigman was able to fulfill her desire for metamorphosis through performance. By dancing the *Hexentanz*, she could realize her search for the *Dasein* and *erleben*: the full coming into being or existence that she felt was the heart of the new dance. But she also recognized that "the power, the magnificence of all creative art lie in knowing how to force chaos into form." Yet, she worked well aware that "the original creative urge was neither weakened nor blocked in the process of molding and shaping." In *The Language of Dance*, Wigman recalls the origins of her dance theme:

Sometimes at night I slipped into the studio and worked myself up into a rhythmic intoxication in order to come closer to the slowly stirring character ... When one night, I returned to my room utterly agitated, I looked into the mirror by chance. What it reflected was the image of one possessed, wild and dissolute, repelling and fascinating. The hair unkempt, the eyes deep in their sockets, the nightgown shifted about, which made the body almost shapeless: there she was – the witch.

(Wigman 1966: 40–1)

The character of the witch allowed the exposure of a part of her personality that she had "never allowed to emerge in such nakedness" (ibid.). She had also mastered the craft of choreographing and thus solidifying such an ephemeral experience, giving definitive form to the physicality and therefore the persona of the Witch. With the addition of the mask she heightened her own experience in performance. Her 1914 Romantic Symbolist representation of a fairy-tale Witch was gone. In its place was a vehicle for genuine change. The desire for an altered state of consciousness in performance was manifested concretely, not theoretically, with the addition of the mask. She wrote of her suffocation within the mask. It sat tightly upon her face, limiting her ability to breathe. The mask also created sensory deprivation by limiting her vision through two narrow eye slits. Orientation in space and balance were both challenged in an extreme way. Through these physical constrictions a new world of possibility for the concert dance was born. In 1933, Rudolph Bach published the definitive reckoning of Wigman's work up to that point. His *Mary Wigman – Werk* placed the *Hexentanz* in the context of her repertory at the height of her career:

> The *Hexentanz* from 1926 can most likely be considered Mary Wigman's most famous work. It truly expresses the summit of her art. Idea, construction of form and interpretation all come together in the *Hexentanz*. It is difficult to decide which dance best exemplifies her art when she has made a steady stream of strong, creative work. Yet the *Hexentanz* emerges as the dance that characterizes the essential elements of her technique.
>
> (Bach 1933: 27)

It is heartening to know that even Mary Wigman's close contemporary Bach was challenged when trying to find a work among the many that defined Wigman's artistic vision. His choice of the *Hexentanz* as such reinforces use of the dance to investigate her practice.

THE MASK AS DOORWAY

Wigman's writings offer a glimpse of what she was looking for when deciding to add the mask to the dance:

> Why should a dancer use a mask? Always when his creative urge causes a split process in him, when his imagination reveals the image of an apparently alien figure which … compels the dancer to a certain kind of metamorphosis. The mask never can and never ought to be an interesting addition or decoration. It must be an essential part of the dance figure, born in a world of visions and transported as if by magic into reality. The mask extinguishes the human being as a person and makes him submit to the fictive figure of the dance.
>
> (Wigman 1973: 124)

The mask has long been recognized as a tool for transformation, initiating entry into the sacred realm. These ideas of masking, while varied, carry across cultures and geographical location. Dutch theologian Gerardus van der Leeuw tied contemporary use of the mask to older ritual, using words that echo Wigman's dance experience:

> The mask belongs to the *sacer ludus* as the great means of stylization. Through it, all events are reduced to a single event, which is at the same time, divine. The mask removes human differentiation from the realm of the accidental and raises it to the divine, eternal and meaningful world of ritual. Through the mask, human action receives a new dimension. It opens a world in which anarchy and possession lie in wait. Whoever puts on a mask is no longer absolutely certain of himself. It might happen that he asks himself which is his true countenance, the mask or his own face.
>
> (van der Leeuw 1963: 84)

Later in life, Wigman explained to a group of students that she chose to wear the mask in the second version of *Hexentanz* to "overcome the individual sphere in order to connect to the archetype" (Partsch-Bergsohn 1994:114). She used the mask for transformation from modern dancer to elemental figure. In this case she became the Witch, embodying what she had described as "stirrings" deep within from her Celtic ancestors.

Following her recognition of these early "stirrings," Wigman had joined in Laban's ritualistic experiments at Monte Verità. She had seen Nolde's studies of masks and ritual objects. Following her first version of *Hexentanz* in 1914, she had experienced the Dada performance practice of using mask and costume to transform the body. For her new version of *Hexentanz*, she added a mask made by Viktor Magito, who was studying the masks of Japanese Noh Theater. Wigman herself describes the decision to use a mask: "And there was still left the first and never used mask of the *Ceremonial Figure*, whose features were my own translated into the demonic." She wrote, "I suddenly knew that fabric [of the costume] and mask ... might give the *Witch Dance* its very own stage image" (Wigman 1966: 41).

At this point, Wigman's many influences came together. Because the 1926 solo contains so many of these artistic elements, *Hexentanz* is like a powerful time capsule. *Hexentanz* also shows today's dancer another way of perceiving the world that holds potential for art making in the future. Wigman's addition of the mask clearly undermined the traditional spectator's position. It can be said to reflect the emergence of the *Neue Sachlichkeit* or new objectivity – the dispassioned arts movement that sprung from the general disillusion following the defeats and horrors of the First World War. By adding the mask, Wigman gave the modern dancer a greater degree of control over the performance experience. The masked Wigman chose to objectify herself as the archetype of the witch and, most importantly, become a vessel for transformation. Within the mask she was able to reveal a face and facets of her personality that were not acceptable in the everyday world.

Only a scant fifty seconds of the 1926 version of *Hexentanz* have been preserved on film. Wigman is first seen as a solo, seated figure. Dressed in a costume made of "fantastic," brocaded, metallic fabric, she has arms, back and feet bare. She wears the face mask, which doesn't hide all of her cheeks, nor does it cover her hair. The eyes appear to be downcast. The overall effect of Magito's mask is almost that of a death mask on a body that is very much alive. The costume and mask help to create an aura of otherworldliness in the dancer.

Writers often consider earlier works through contemporary lenses. The dance works of the early moderns have been used as examples of the rising feminist spirit. These modern forebears are easily carried into these analogies because of their gender and the revolutionary times in which they lived. Wigman referenced the female identity when she described the discovery of the character of the witch in *Hexentanz*, asking, "... isn't a bit of a witch hidden in every hundred-percent female, no matter which form its origin may have?" (Wigman 1966: 41). For Wigman, becoming the Witch was a uniquely personal experience, one that placed her in a position of power as a performer, beyond gender, within the realm of shaman and artist.

HEXENTANZ: A DESCRIPTION

As the space fills with a hard, white light, Wigman is first seen as a solo, seated figure surrounded by darkness. She sits on the floor directly facing the audience with her feet planted in front of her and knees upright under the fabric of the costume. Her hands cover the masked face as her fingers stretch wide. They grasp the space before the face, pulling apart as if opening an invisible curtain. The tension in the arms and hands is so great as to cause the hands to vibrate as if pressing an invisible wall that separates dancer from audience. From this slow, tensed opening gesture, movement explodes. It begins with a sharp rapping motion of the left hand, as if the dancer were knocking on the door of a forbidden passageway, again, the space between dancer and spectator. The percussive movement of the arms and hands corresponds to the percussive sound of the score. Indeed it is the movement that initiates the sound. Because the movement slightly anticipates each percussive note, it appears to generate the very sound itself.

From this opening percussive movement, tension is released, the hands soften, circling and gathering force in front of the masked face. This conjuring movement is resolved as she places her hands on upright knees. A slow circling of the upper body begins, with each circle resolving in a drawing inward of the body and a sharp look forward, as if a spell is being cast out toward the audience.

The second circling concludes with a downward focus to the center of the dancer. The hands begin to pry the legs open by pressing outward from the inner knees. Here is a source of the Witch's power. The internal focus of Wigman and the slow tempo create a sense of effort and deliberation. Once the knees are opened, she begins a forward, keening ripple that initiates from the center of the abdomen. Circling the upper body over the grounded and opened thighs, each revolution resolves in a sharp thrust of the body, arms and facial focus outward to the left diagonal. There is a sense of increasing urgency as the tempo increases and another sound, the crash of a cymbal, is added to the score.

Then, silence. The right hand slowly, softly circles toward the face and opens out with a reach to the right. The hand returns to the face again, this time nearly caressing the lips and then unfolding, as if performing a benediction or bestowing absolution. For Wigman this gesture carried the hermetic authority of the Sphinx that she referred to, adding the caution to "Keep the secret." The moment of quiet dissolves into mounting tension. The clawed hands reach up together and the focus follows, looking upward as if gathering divine power. Abruptly, the moment is broken as the arms gather toward each other, cross and grasp the knees. Wigman's mastery of time and tension are fully revealed in this moment. The heavy, pregnant tension of the upward reach is ruptured by the lightning movement of the hands and arms. Upward to downward, outward to inward, the dichotomy and contrast of movement qualities is shocking. The silence is broken with a loud crash of cymbals as the hands clasp the knees and the focus shoots directly toward the audience.

The seated figure then begins her assault. Gaining momentum in movement and sound, she shifts from hip to hip, rocking as the hands sequentially reach from knee to knee. The tempo continues to increase as the dancer takes this rocking into a forward locomotion. She strikes out directly toward the audience, reaching with each leg until, grasping both ankles, she pounds her feet on the floor in front of her. With a loud crash, everything stops for a moment. From this brief stillness, the dancer begins to revolve, still seated, while her feet beat out a tattoo as if the floor was the head of a drum. After one eight-count revolution, the pace increases to double time; the feet become a blur and then she suddenly stops with the right leg extended. The final movement that was captured on film is a look over the extended right foot of the dancer that becomes a slow, sweeping gaze.

In *Hexentanz*, the use of sharp, percussive sound punctuates the aggressive movement. The solo figure seems to generate the sound, controlling the environment and all of those within it. Even in the silence filled with a single, slowly fluid gesture, the tension is palpable. The silence is resolved with a percussive slap of sound and movement. From the opening position through the final look toward the audience, Wigman creates a tension that never diminishes in intensity. Even the moments of softening gesture radiate the figure's absolute control over the time and the space. The vocabulary of movement that Wigman created for the dance is unfamiliar and yet specific to the emotions evoked. Power, tension and control are present in each gesture and shape. The construction of this opening of the dance is simple. The dancer never leaves the floor in the first minute of the work. Instead of detracting from the effect, the simplicity adds to the power of the statement. The dancer remains in control of the movement, not carried away by it.

The figure is neither malevolent nor benevolent; it is omnipotent. Throughout *Hexentanz*, sound, movement, mask and costume are unified in intent. The dance presents a mythical creature who has power over those watching. The audience can no longer feel safe. She becomes the Witch and spectators are in danger of becoming bewitched by her. She is a timeless force, embodying pure power. The dance is one of a fully mature woman who recognizes the strength of her sensuality.

In the *Witch Dance*, Wigman was able to synthesize the previous dozen years of her life as a dance artist, including ideas concerning the use or non-use of music in dance that grew from her exposure to Dalcroze's music and movement theories. She crafted carefully, using ideas she had explored with Laban: the paradoxical and synchronous coupling of rational crafting with the flight into the mythic and ritual. Even the Sphinx-like gesture of touching fingers to masked lips crept into the character of the Witch from the Freemasonic practices at Monte Verità. Such imagery is still present in hermetic Masonic texts. Wigman said that the gesture was meant to "keep the secret" – presumably of the Masonic rites and of larger forces. Wigman also drew on masked Dada experiments that distorted the gestalt in performance, and contributed ultimately to the deliberate development of her own distinctive performance persona. Describing the Elemental Dance Composition, she embraced the grotesque and this was a manifestation of "everything apparitional, spectral, whether confined to earthy or released to transcendental experiences" (Wigman 1973: 92). Certainly, she made dances on many themes from the sublime to the anguished, but the potential of the grotesque for danced expression was one of Wigman's most radical visions.

Before Mary Wigman, Isadora Duncan had unleashed such energy in her *Furies*, as had Gluck in his *Orpheus*. *Sleeping Beauty*'s wicked Carabosse had epitomized grotesque and evil forces in the ballet and the narratives of the *Ballets Russes* were filled with unusual heroes and villains. In all of these earlier representations, the grotesque appeared in contrast, diametrically opposed to what was good and beautiful. Wigman's grotesque witch appears somehow more personal, less caricature or literary figure and more immediate. She makes no apologies for allowing herself to revel in the shadow side of human nature – of her own nature. She wrote: "All sensations of anxiety, all chaotic conditions of despair arising from torment, hatred, or fury, grow in this medium of expression up to and beyond the boundaries of the purely human and blend themselves with inhuman, demoniacal violence" (ibid.: 93). The effect was shocking, certainly. But the fact that this aspect of human nature could be revealed and communicated through performance was revolutionary. Wigman spoke about the performance of the *Hexentanz* as possessing her in a profoundly elemental way. She recalled the Witch "with her unrestrained, naked instincts, with her insatiable lust for life, beast and woman at one and the same time" (Wigman 1966: 41). Remembering the emergence of the character, Wigman said, "I shuddered at my own image, at the exposure of this facet of my ego which I had never allowed to emerge in such unashamed nakedness" (ibid.). In this, the *Hexentanz* may be the definitive solo of early *Ausdruckstanz*.

GROUP DANCE

Wigman accomplished much as a soloist inside and outside of Germany. But she also aspired to choreograph for an ensemble. Wigman saw the group dance as retaining the essential characteristics of the solo. For the choreographer, the group dance also permitted an amplified use of the formal elements of space, time and energy. Multiple dancing bodies permitted more variety and capacity for change. When she writes of the demands of creating an ensemble work, we hear her own struggles to form a dance group and simultaneously keep the solo dance alive. She described the role of a dancer as twofold: "on the one hand, perfecting the dance personality as an individual; and on the other hand, blending this individuality with an ensemble" (Wigman 1973: 129). She believed that the young dancers of her era had a strong feeling for a common cause that supported ensemble dance. But she also saw that the drive for self-expression must be handled with understanding and patience in order to protect and develop the individual talent. The abilities that group members brought were to be cultivated within the framework of the dances themselves. Thus, self-expression would not come into conflict with the teamwork necessary to work in a dance ensemble.

Dance talent manifests itself in two ways, she said. The first was what she termed the "productive" talent that arises from creative imagination. This talent emerges as having a real mind of its own with which it adapts training to its own original purposes. Along with the ability to modify training material, such talent exerts the power to influence others through initiative and qualities of leadership. From this pool of talent she identified choreographers, managers, composers and soloists. Wigman reflected on these leadership qualities in her 1927 essay "Dance and the Modern Woman," written in English for *The Dancing Times* of London. Her adoption of this *Führer* principle certainly predated the rise of the Third Reich and consolidated as her work with other dancers developed. This progression of choreographic control mirrors the evolution of Martha Graham's leadership role, which solidified in her own dance ensembles and through the codification of her technique. It is worthwhile to consider the development of the innate qualities of the choreographer in the light of Wigman's career. While she could comment on the task of the choreographer from her own experience, she also knew that the so-called choreographic or productive path was not for all dancers.

In contrast or in complement to the productive talent, Wigman termed a second type of dance talent "reproductive." Such talent was innate to those dancers who became ideal instruments for the creative forces and visions of choreographers. And she made it clear that these dancers had gifts all of their own. With the reproductive talent comes the genius for absorbing and carrying to fruition the ideas of others. This requires a critical insight derived from shrewd observation and an intellect capable of penetration into motivations, metaphors and meanings. For these dancers, Wigman saw their professional potential best realized through the challenges of dancing with a group, but not merely as instruments of the choreographer. These artists were called on to use a strength of personality that would be neither subverted nor stifled by working with others.

In 1921, Wigman choreographed her first major-length group work, *The Seven Dances of Life*. Among the dancers rehearsing the work were Berthe Trümpy, Yvonne Georgi and Gret Palucca. Opening night was almost cancelled at the last moment because Palucca suffered a foot injury that required surgery and dancer Birgit Nohr also was injured. New ensemble member Trümpy stepped into Palucca's part and danced alongside Wigman with Hilde Daeves, Lena Hanke and Georgi. Together, they made dance history.

THE SEVEN DANCES OF LIFE (1921)

On 1 October 1921, Mary Wigman presented a work she had chor-eographed for producer Hanns Niedecken-Gebhard, a dramaturge inter-ested in expanding the role of the dance within opera performance. He and Wigman had known each other since the days at Monte Verità, and now Wigman's choreography for his production of *The Rose in Love's Garden* firmly established their long friendship. With Palucca, she struggled with the "corseted" dancers at the Stattsopera in Hanover (Müller 1986a: 90). Lured by the idea of theater work, but frustrated by the necessity of working with ballet-trained dancers, Wigman would soon have the opportunity to craft and direct a work that was totally her own. On 14 December 1921, Niedecken-Gebhard produced Wigman's first evening-length performance for her small ensemble. *The Seven Dances of Life* premiered at the Opera House in Frankfurt. The first half of the evening was dedicated to performance of a Mozart operetta, *Basten and Bastienne*. Wigman and her cast took the stage after the intermission.

Figure 13 *Dance of Suffering* from *The Seven Dances of Life*, 1921. Dancers from left: Yvonne Georgi, Mary Wigman, Gret Palucca, Hilde Daeves. Photograph by Alexa Ritter, courtesy of the Tanzarchiv Berlin

The Seven Dances of Life may have debuted that evening, but the performance was the culmination of years of analysis, study and self-discovery. In that wonderful, horrible and formative year of 1918–19 Wigman had written the poem that became the libretto for the dance. And her extant sketches for the dance vividly illustrate how she labored over the symbolic content and choreographic form of the work. She undertook this project while recovering from a physical and emotional breakdown. While she was a patient in the tuberculosis sanatorium in the Engadin region of the Swiss Alps, *The Seven Dances of Life* was her creative refuge. It is also a map of her struggle to persist in dedicating her life to dance against all odds. And it is clearly derivative of the experimental works that she had been cast in by Laban.

The year 1918 was the end of her association with Laban. That year he fashioned *The Sultan's Grimace: A Dance Play in Five Scenes*. It was one of the "oriental" fairy-tale pantomimes that he made during his tenure in Zurich. Certainly, many dancers took on "Orientalist" themes, imitating such dance luminaries as Ruth St. Denis and Maud Allen. It has been suggested that Wigman modeled *The Seven Dances of Life* after Allen's work, but Allen's *Salome* had initially made a stir in 1907, more than a decade before Wigman began to work on her *Seven Dances*. It seems likely that Wigman was developing a dramatic piece that had a direct relationship to her final period under Laban's tutelage. The trappings of *The Sultan's Grimace* hold many elements found in *The Seven Dances of Life*. In Laban's work there appeared a Sultan/ruler, a female slave whose dance held the power to save lives, attending dancers, a dervish dancer and an executioner. There was a large throne upon which the Sultan sat as ruler and cloth handkerchiefs that were used as props symbolizing transition and choice. However, where *The Sultan's Grimace* appears as more of a social comedy, in which disguises and mistaken identities drive the plot, Wigman's *The Seven Dances of Life* is earnestly serious and more in the tradition of **Sturm und Drang**, but with an uplifting outcome.

Sturm und Drang movement – literally Storm and Stress, this movement of the late 1700s was the zenith of German romanticism. *Sturm und Drang* writers and artists such as Goethe saw the human quest for perfectibility as impossible, yet the only worthwhile aim for creative genius. The movement can be characterized as a revolt against Enlightenment rationalism and the early stages of industrialization.

By the time that she was to set the work in 1921, many other influences had entered Wigman's creative life. Besides having a group of dancers dedicated to working with her, she had also embarked on a romantic relationship with psychiatrist and art historian Hanns Prinzhorn. She had known Prinzhorn since her days at Hellerau, when he had been engaged to her roommate Erna Hoffman. While Wigman was working with Laban during the years of the First World War, Prinzhorn was gathering and cataloging a unique collection of art works done by patients at psychiatric hospitals. Led by the head of the Psychiatric Department at the University in Heidelberg, he went on to publish a richly illustrated book, *The Artistry of the Mentally Ill*. His groundbreaking book not only documented the art collection but also interpreted and contextualized the artwork. His writing is a phenomenological critique of the prevailing culture that disparaged such "insane art." He argued not only that many of the works therein had genuine artistic quality, but also that the creators of the works deserved a positive re-evaluation in the light of such artistic merit. While his scientific colleagues were reserved in their reaction, artists were enthusiastic. Jean Dubuffet was highly inspired by the works, and coined the term "Outsider Art" to legitimize these artists in the world of aesthetic pursuits. Indeed, for many artists working in the Expressionist style, Prinzhorn's work was a welcome validation of their own artistic impulses and Wigman was among them. Wigman and Prinzhorn saw in each other a kindred spirit with a unique depth of insight into their own pursuits. Extant correspondence between them is passionate and poetic. On 3 March 1921, Prinzhorn began a poem to Wigman with the words "Dance in Holy Life." Equally an Expressionist tome and Romantic love poem, it speaks of the vessel of her body holding the "thousand wild forms that sound the one blessed chord of life," behind which "death stands seething dressed in black yet the body sings of this holy life!" The imagery in Prinzhorn's poem was fully realized through Wigman's dance wherein the Dance of Life follows the Dance of Death (Prinzhorn 1921).

Besides her relationship with Prinzhorn, many other of her early influences were woven into the fabric of *The Seven Dances of Life*. These influences included ideas from Eastern philosophy that she pursued at

Hellerau, Laban's experiments in defining the fundamental elements of dance as well as his Freemasonic practices and dramatic theatrical values. The dance also reflects the existential struggle found in **Goethe**'s great epic *Faust* and Wigman's ongoing identification with Goethe's writing. In her biography of Wigman, Hedwig Müller dedicates many pages to facsimiles of Wigman's notes and detailed drawings for the dance, and any deeper analysis would be well served by looking at these pages. They include drawings of the pathways through space done in Wigman's own hand, with detailed description of the costumes and staging. Müller also makes a brilliant case for Wigman's incorporation of Goethe's color theory in her choice of costume color for each section. Such symbolism runs deeply under the surface of Wigman's carefully crafted dance drama. The dance was a mystic composition. When describing the intention of such mystic dances, she clearly stated that she was not creating a tribal or ritual dance, nor representing a singular religious idea. She writes:

> We may call a dance mystic when it is symbolic of cosmic powers in its expression and form, when the personal life experience of the choreographer yields to the dance visualization of the incomprehensible and eternal. The mystic dance presupposes the choreographer's personal maturity.
>
> (Wigman 1973: 93)

Johann Wolfgang von Goethe (1749–1832) – one of the greatest thinkers in Western culture; best known as a poet and philosopher, but his scientific, aesthetic and musical ideas were enormously influential. His best-known works were *Sorrows of Young Werther*, *Wilhelm Meister's Apprenticeship* and **Faust**, in which human mortality, the scientific enterprise and the nature of spiritual longing are major themes.

By 1921, Wigman had already choreographed and performed dozens of shorter dances and several dedicated to "oriental" themes, but in *The Seven Dances of Life*, her philosophy is remarkably laid bare. Her skill as a choreographer and performer would continue to develop, yet *The Seven Dances of Life* appears as a manifesto of Wigman's beliefs. It is also reminiscent of a modern morality play, close to the great medieval tradition of performing the spiritual trials of "Everyman," or importantly in this case, of Everywoman. Faced with the obstacles of being a female iconoclast, Wigman naturally identified her life in dance as a calling coming from a higher source. And from that source she could claim cosmic support for her own creative genius and ambitions.

THE SEVEN DANCES OF LIFE

Characters in the Dance:

The Speaker, The Solo Dancer, A Group of Four Female Dancers, Two Drummers.

In *The Mary Wigman Book*, Walter Sorell translated Wigman's description of the opening of the dance drama:

> Music sounds softly, as if coming from afar. The sounds tremble in space ... The flute sings wistfully ... It dreams of tenderness and love, of happiness and suffering, of ever new desires; then it merges into the singing of the strings, which grows louder and crescendos into a deafening cry of life. – All sounds fade out. Only a single dance rhythm flickers back and forth, lightly and fleetingly ... Then there is silence ... and the dark space still vibrates [with] the memory of it all.

In the silence,

> A figure steps in front of the curtain; a man wrapped in a huge cape, hardly visible in the half-dark which seems to light up slowly with the sound of his voice. While he speaks, the strings gently accompany him. They whisper like cicadas on the meadows on a hot summer day, a thin, uninterrupted singing sound.
>
> (Wigman 1973: 72 – modified from Sorell's translation)

MARY WIGMAN'S TEXT

The Prologue of the Speaker
The King spoke: "You dance to save your life,
Slave!
And if your dance
Can explain to me
Life's meaning,
Then you will go free."
And the woman danced

the first Dance of Life,
the Dance of unfulfilled Longing
"Loosen her from her shackles,"
said the King.
And the woman
danced the Dance of Love.
"Do not kill her yet,"
shouted the King.
At that the woman danced
the wild Dance of Lust,
breaking out of her shackles
and going beyond all confines.
The King covered his head:
"You will have to die for that,
Woman!"
And the slaves brought
the black veil of death.
But the dancer paid no attention
And danced past them
in the Dance of Suffering.
And then she danced the dark Dance
Of the Demon,
Stirring up all forces
Lying dormant and hidden in life.
And when the dance was done,
she bowed before the King:
"I am ready, my lord."
And she began to dance
The silent Dance of Death.
Again the slaves lifted
The veil of death
to cover her with it forever.
But the King
kissed the dancer's forehead
and said:
"Your dance conquered Life
and it conquered Death.
Now Live and be free!"
    (Wigman in Müller 1986a: 92–3)

[In the following description, quotation marks and block quotes denote translations of selections from Wigman's sketchbook in Müller 1986a and Sorell 1986.]

At the end of this speech, the orchestra "shouts with joy." The opening lighting is "warm and golden" and reminiscent of the solar imagery found in descriptions of performances at Monte Verità and written in Nietzsche's *Zarathustra*. And, in keeping with her emphatic belief that sound must be integral to the dance, two drummers are crouched in the downstage left and right corners. With their steady blows the action begins, and with the strike of a gong, four female dancers enter. They walk and run with small, precise steps penetrating the space with straight and curved pathways. After a deep bow, they slowly open the curtain revealing a "fantastic figure," a larger-than-life-size effigy of the King. This huge puppet is resplendent, "an idol in gold," and seated on a large, richly carved throne. There is a platform made of three steps that lead to the throne and Mary Wigman is lying stretched along the bottom step. Shining in a silver gown, she rises as "the garment trickles down her limbs like fluid water."

Thus she began the **Dance of Longing**. Longing for what? With her dance she describes her longing to live life fully, to dance unrestrained and to make a place for her beloved dance in the larger world. Metaphorically, the King had chained her. The figure of the King is not a man or even alive. This effigy appears as an allegorical figure symbolizing all the dominating figures and forces of her past, and perhaps those dominant forces ever present in the world. Wigman used a restrained, wave-like motif that rippled through her body. With her focus turned inward, she danced what she termed a deep yearning that proved her salvation. As the other dancers brought her before the throne, her arms were released as her chains were loosened.

And with more freedom, she began the **Dance of Love**. Set in 3/4 time, the full orchestra supported her waltzing figure. Described as "cheerful, beaming and warm, with small absurd-humorous movements and some brief sentimentality," the dance builds from a light, floating motif into the "passion of a big swing." In the spoken prelude, this Dance of Love caused the King to shout, "Do not kill her yet!" But then, with a clang of the gong, the scene changes. The **Dance of Lust** begins. Bright light fills the space. To the sound of beating drums, Wigman rushes around, flying across the stage with wide jumps. Against "wildly rhythmic drumming and howling gongs, the body of the dancer raves and blazes in a self-generating glow." Spiraling through the space and spinning in counter directions she moves from high to low levels in deep turns and high jumps until she pounces into the middle of the stage. With short runs from the corners, the four dancers join her. At the strike of the gong they all run and turn, forming a moving mandala that spirals outward to the four corners of the stage and then condenses by drawing all dancers to the center. This motif is repeated three times and on the fourth repetition the supporting dancers leave, while Wigman slows her spinning and travels to the center. The instruments reach a crescendo – a musical rendering of the King's shout that "You will have to die for that Woman!" In the center of the space she "staggers, reels and falls." In Wigman's scenario, the King and society made no room for such passion, irrationality and abandon especially for a woman, this woman.

So from the Dance of Lust began the **Dance of Suffering**. Here is Wigman's representation of *Opfer*, the sacrifice required of an individual, which in this case becomes the trials necessary to realize one's destiny. And for Wigman such sacrifice would be made for the dance. Wigman had danced a section entitled *Opfer* (Sacrifice) in her *Ecstatic Dances* of 1917. In 1931, she would devote an entire dance cycle to the theme of *Opfer*, which would become one of her most successful programs. In *The Seven Dances of Life*, grief, suffering and sacrifice are required for her very survival. As the curtain opens on this section, the four supporting dancers enter gravely. They carry a black funerary veil as a symbol of the ultimate limitation that all human beings face. They spread the cloth on the floor and kneel at the edges. The drums are quiet. The drummers cover their faces. Yet Mary Wigman smiles and quietly steps onto the black cloth. With the other dancers as witnesses, she begins to move with "limbs heavy with grief ... with deep heavy gestures and a slow rotation, with spiraling arms, she sinks slowly to the ground." The dancers embrace the fallen figure. From this silent tableau, a deep ringing fills the room with crystal clear sound. The four girls leave and Wigman is left alone.

The **Dance of the Demon** begins with a poem by Wigman. It is the first time that the Narrator's voice has been heard – the first text to interrupt the dance action – since the Prologue:

I was –
I am, –
I will be, –

You became aware of me
on one day of your life.
Shapeless, I wafted
through the spheres of
the world.
But you created me,
You gave me the form
In which I now
Dwell in your life.
What could make you
fear me?
[Am I] not that agent
between nothingness and
being?
Why are you frightened
Of the creation of your own
fantasy?
I come to you
in those lost hours
when life is silent.

Wigman remains still. Crouching in the upstage right corner, she seems to wake when the recitation of the *Song of the Demon* dies away. Then she slowly comes to life as if the words have penetrated her dancing body. She gradually rises, creeping along the ground with short rhythmic steps. Then she jumps up and dances. Divided into three distinct sections, most of the dance is done in silence. Her body determines the rhythm. There are abrupt changes from slow to quick time. Accents happen while she is jumping. And these jumps are bound, with the legs tucked into the body and with a sense of being contained and pulled downward rather than releasing upward and outward into the air. The first part of the dance ends as Wigman sinks to the floor, with her body rigid, frozen in stillness while the air fills with the sound of tolling bells and gongs.

The second part of the dance is described as uncanny and grotesque. It is also danced in silence. The dancer moves as if she has sunk deeply into the ground. Time and again she is pulled down "to be reborn time and again, being the same and always different." Finally, the bells sound once again and Wigman returns to the floor.

I carry you through worlds
concealed from the eyes of
man.
I lift you to heights
Which your human eye
can never measure.
I pour
of that life into your veins
of which man must die, if the demon
does not protect him.
You will no longer be without me.
And would you ever want
to miss those dark hours
when your eyes have learned
to see more than can be seen?
When my powers penetrated you
and you became one
with the elements?
Beloved!

The last part of the dance becomes a desperate search. Despairing, tortured by inner conflict, the dancer's steps and movements are huge, excessive and filled with "twitching desire" and distorted beauty. As if in a wicked dream, the dance recreates the realm of sleepless nights and dreams and ghostly images.

The smile of horror
around your red lips
makes me thirsty.
I feed
on your warm blood –
Now I am quite close to you!
Do you feel
how the invisible dance
of my limbs holds you embraced? –
I was, –
I am, –
I will be,–
Before you,

Figure 14 Mary Wigman in *Dance of the Demon* from *The Seven Dances of Life*, 1921. Photograph by Nino Hess, Frankfurt, courtesy of the Tanzarchiv Berlin

with you,
after you, imperishable …
(Wigman 1973: 78–9)

At the end, the dancer disappears into the dark side stage as if the ground has swallowed her. She has absorbed the power unleashed in the cycle up to this moment. The space is empty but the music continues to flow through the room in warm waves. The oppression of the previous section lifts.

The music fades and in the silence, Wigman again returns to the stage. She stands alone. She walks with deep and controlled steps as the drummers leave the stage. Wigman opens the curtain to the effigy of the King and bows her head. The four dancers enter with torches lit and place them at the front of the stage. Torchlight is the only light in the room. She dances the **Dance of Death** with silent resolve. This dance is described as an absolutely solemn ceremony. It ends with Wigman sinking and kneeling before the throne until her forehead touches the ground. The four dancers place the black veil around her shoulders and she is carried off stage.

Yet she enters again. For the final **Dance of Life** she is clothed in a gleaming golden dress, "shining like the sun." Smiling, she gestures for the other dancers to join her and she flings her arms wide open. The orchestra fills the space with "joyful music" and light floods the stage returning it to the warm glow of the opening scene. Wigman and the dancers respond by opening apart with impetus. Using big, swinging movements they travel in curved pathways. Their high runs are punctuated by turning jumps. They move in unison both in their gestures and in their spatial patterns, using great energy and a joyfulness that reaches toward ecstasy. The dancers come together in a circle. Her notes declare:

Give me your hands. Let us dance together the dance of all dances! Are we not dancers of life? Do we not carry the knowledge of life in ourselves? And do we not carry the full knowledge of life in our dance? Let us sing the dancing beauty of the limbs and of life – the most divine dance, the dance of all dances!

(Sorell 1986: 77)

The Seven Dances of Life still stands as Wigman's own "dance of all dances." As a symbolic rendering of her own life's philosophy, it can offer a window into one important region of the constituent values that guided her life and work.

The King had said:

"Your dance conquered Life
and it conquered Death.
Now Live and be Free!"

Under such a banner of freedom, Wigman pursued her choreographic path. While the pursuit was personal, she had come to realize that, in order to expand her dance repertory, she had to be aware of the larger forces that shaped choreographic processes and greater trends in the dance world at large. Along with solo dances such as the *Hexentanz* and works like *The Seven Dances of Life* in which she incorporated her professional group, the mass choric dance had become an integral part of the dance life of her time.

CHORIC DANCE

The principles demanded by the choric dance are born of the needs that arise when moving large numbers of dancing bodies. When considering the choric dance, we can chart a progression from the idiosyncratic movement allowed in the dance solo through the cooperative cohesion of the group dance and the final development of mass unison in the choric. The key feature of the choric dance is that of simplicity of movement. Each dancer's postures and gestures must be pared down to a united expression that creates an impact due to its mass volume rather than technical virtuosity. However, within this form there is room for individual interpretation within the prescribed movement phrases. Demanding group awareness, shared movement qualities and rhythmic unison were vital to the execution of such gestures. While not always the practice of amateurs, the choric dance did lend itself to non-professionals. In 1937, Hanya Holm made her masterwork *Trend* at Bennington College. She carried her experience of working with Wigman to the American stage. Choreographing for thirty-three dancers, many of them students, she imported Wigman's choric methods to make a dance statement of great impact. Following the performance, Alwin Nikolais wrote, "... the mass of dancers, just by raising one hand together blew off the whole top of the universe" (Kriegsman 1981: 165).

This is not to say that the choreographer's task in the choric dance is a simple one. Instead of movement invention for individual dancers, the emphasis is placed on the elements of time and spatial structure. Not only does the grouping of dancers in the space create an architecture of bodies but also it reveals dynamic tensions between the groups. Space remains an invisible partner, but one that links groups of dancers rather than the soloist to the cosmos. Expressions of unity or opposition are realized through these spatial relationships. While every individual movement is enlarged through working in union with the group, the rhythmic content is also amplified through use of unison and mass. In theory, Wigman had a mastery of these concepts. In 1930 she was asked to make the concepts into concrete form in the *Totenmal*.

TOTENMAL (1930)

Wigman had been approached by Albert Talhoff to choreograph for the cast of more than fifty lay dancers for *Totenmal*. In her attempt to keep up with the trend toward choric works, Wigman took up the challenge. However, her own writing reveals that she viewed her goal not as the creation of mass movement but more as an experiment in uniting dance with the spoken word. Talhoff had anchored the work in his chanted poetry performed by a mass *Sprech-chor* or speaking chorus, which dictated the movements of the dancers along with the shadings of underlying feelings. Wigman saw this undertaking as a natural outgrowth of her mission, not only to create a *Gesamkunstwerk*, but also to prove dance an art form of equal stature to theater. Wigman had cut her pre-professional teeth on opera, performing Gluck's *Orpheus and Eurydice* at the Dalcroze School. Since those early days, she had labored to bring dance to the fore, no longer subordinate to music. But in truth, Wigman lacked the practical experience to direct such a large amateur group. Since those early experiments at Monte Verità and her separation from Laban, she had pursued a professional career distinguished by solos and smaller group works. Given the complexity of making *Totenmal*, Wigman fell back on theories of the movement choir that she had earlier explored with Laban.

While photos allow a glimpse of still shapes from sections in the work, they disguise the overall sweep and style of movement. In keeping with her experiments of the late 1920s, Wigman did employ wooden masks made by Bruno Goldschmitt that gave individual character to members of the women's chorus, comprised primarily of her trained dancers. For the mass of amateur men, the war dead, she used masks that appear individual in countenance yet uniform in effect. Photos reveal her grouping these dancers together architecturally to shape the performance space. The choruses also served to frame and respond to Wigman's solo dance and her struggling duet with a figure that signified the malevolence of war. The dance was to be performed through the summer following the Third Dancers' Congress. After the showing of *Totenmal* in rehearsal, it became clear that the work was a critical failure, despite the collaboration of so many well-known artists and the investment of considerable economic resources. Such extravagance in Germany's desperately depressed economy, coupled with the disappointing outcome of the performance, drew outspoken criticism. *Schrifttanz* editor Alfred Schlee called the performance a sad confirmation of the flood of dilettantism that was destroying the new dance, ironically echoing Wigman's own doubts about the state of dance training.

While the Third Congress and the production of *Totenmal* seemed a failure on many levels, it also appeared that *Ausdruckstanz* was in a state of decline. In truth the entire infrastructure of the German Republic was in chaos and cultural elements such as the German dance reflected the critical state of affairs. Submitting to the choric dance and using amateurs for the performance shows, Wigman was caught amidst desire and necessity, idealism and peer pressure. In her later writing, she appears philosophical about the critical failure of *Totenmal*. She insisted that the entire project was an unprecedented experiment to wed the dance with the spoken word. And it was. For Wigman, the amateurs presented a challenge to be borne for the sake of experimentation. Her company, trained in her own technique, had been disbanded due to lack of funding, leaving only a small core led by Holm to anchor the women's chorus in *Totenmal*.

Susan Manning has proposed *Totenmal* as a prototype for the Nazi spectacles to come. Manning's argument appears particularly concrete in consideration of Talhoff's later commitment to National Socialism and Wigman's work under the regime. However, she allows that "most contemporary spectators considered *Totenmal* a pacifist statement" (Manning 1993: 159). *Totenmal* also can be considered a modernist statement in its pluralism: Talhoff's text included letters from British and French soldiers, as well as Germans. This surprising lack of

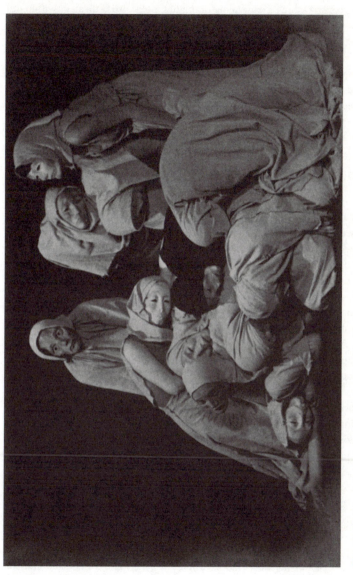

Figure 15 Women's Chorus from *Totenmal*, 1930. Photographer unknown, courtesy of the Tanzarchiv Berlin

nationalism, which Elizabeth Selden termed "supranationalism," may be construed as "concealing a highly politicized theater within an apolitical aura" (ibid.: 160). However, it could also be viewed as a statement of solidarity among all combatants and all mourners. No *völkisch*, nature myths appear. Instead, the work reflects a sad sweep of history and the universal misery of warfare. For Wigman, it was a continuation of her mission to use *Ausdruckstanz* to express the human condition. But in truth the human condition was becoming inextricably intertwined with the political order, for such is the nature of totalitarianism.

FINAL SOLO CONCERT

Twelve years passed between the experiment of *Totenmal* and Wigman's final solo concert. Since *Totenmal*, she had experienced great successes beyond the borders of Germany and she had choreographed and performed as part of the 1936 nationalist Olympic spectacle. She had also fallen into disillusionment and despair amid personal and professional losses. Wigman had often declared that she would choose to retire from the stage before her performance powers declined. About the same time that she lost her Dresden studio, Wigman presented her final solo concert in February 1942.

As was her practice, the works in this concert grew from improvisatory sessions with her composer at the time, Aleida Montijn. Together they developed the dance themes. The performance included her *Farewell and Thanksgiving*, which was captured on film. In fact, the government supported documentation of this final performance. The film proves that Wigman was still in command of her dancing and also shows her mastery of using motif to build gestural language. She repeats a rippling movement that reverberates through her upper body and along her arm, to the tips of her fingers. Reminiscent of a farewell wave, the gesture is not charged with tension but rather with a sort of yielding, an appreciative acceptance of an inescapable departure. But the movement also speaks of an emotion that was intended to continue beyond that moment of leave taking. Even on film, the surrounding space appears charged and she draws her focus inward in a sort of moving benediction. Then her gaze follows her hand and she looks out beyond the performance space. After one of her last performances, an audience member reportedly approached Wigman,

"Mary Wigman, it was more beautiful than ever. But it is dangerous for you. Too many tears have been shed in the audience" (Wigman in Rannow and Stabel 1994: 57).

Isa Partsch-Bergsohn recalls being moved to tears by another dance in Wigman's farewell concert. "*The Dance of Niobe* moved me deeply. It had nothing of the pathos and literalness of the first dance [*The Dance of Brunhilde*] but abstractly condensed desperation ..." (Partsch-Bergshon 1994: 112). Wigman was able to dance her own anguish through the character of Niobe. In literature, the earliest mention of Niobe, in Homer, had come to represent a stock form of bereavement. Niobe is the mother forever mourning her slain children. She is a matriarch whose overarching pride left her blind to her own limitations against the infinite power of the gods. In the end, wearied with the shedding of her tears, Niobe was turned to stone. Wigman used her dance theme to express her new reckoning of the political reality. In many ways, Wigman's dances were her children, borne of her calling to prove the dance art a great and profound vehicle of the human spirit. That such a calling could be subverted, co-opted and misguided, and finally rejected had been unimaginable in the cosmology of the young Mary Wigman. However, in her diary she had written, "The unthinkable has become reality; we have war" (Wigman Diary entry, 4 September 1939). After the Battle of Stalingrad, she responded with the new dance:

> I just had to do something about it, maybe only to get rid of my own feelings. So I started this dance, dedicated to women in the war. It started with a haughty feeling, as if to challenge the gods ... I remember there is a figure in Greek myth who has gone through all this. It was Niobe. The dance begins with a challenge to the gods in the pride of women, then the movements are more quiet, thinking of the wonderful time when the baby was born ... Then it goes back to the challenge; then she gives her children away; then she receives the wound of an arrow through her own heart as she ... mourns over her children; then she [Wigman in the dance] sits again on her stool, emptiness turned into stone as Niobe was turned into stone.

> (Wigman 1973: 163)

Figure 16 *Dance of Niobe* from Mary Wigman's farewell performance, 1942.
Photographer unknown, courtesy the Tanzarchiv Berlin

4

PRACTICAL EXERCISES

This final section outlines a series of practical exercises, with particular attention to Wigman's pedagogy. These exercises are intended to give the experimenter a visceral experience of the performance and training elements that appear most crucial to understanding Mary Wigman's viewpoint. The exercises are not intended to recreate Mary Wigman's teaching practice. They are simply one contemporary way of experiencing the fundamental elements identified by Wigman as she formulated her deep exploration into the stuff that dance is made of. An appreciation for the uniqueness of Wigman's German dance came to me through an American modern dancer. Eve Gentry joined Hanya Holm's original dance company in 1936 and worked with Holm during those formative years of modern dance as a performer and teacher at Holm's studio. As an American dancer in the 1980s and 1990s, Gentry revealed to me values and methodology that seemed at once revolutionary and part of a dance legacy that had been lost to many contemporary dancers. Ongoing research and the generosity of many former Wigman students allowed me to continue to learn about Wigman's methods even after Gentry passed away in 1994. These exercises developed from a burning desire to understand Mary Wigman's philosophy, to share her concepts with current dance and theater students and to recognize the lasting significance of her work. Some exercises may seem familiar to students of theater and dance improvisation. In each exercise, the emphasis is on the underlying concept as it relates to Wigman's fundamentals.

> Did I comprehend at all at that time what Laban had in mind? I was young and impatient, I wanted to dance, I wanted to create and communicate something that concerned other people too. What was a theory to me? I believe that the foundations of my career as a dancer as well as a dance pedagogue were laid in those few weeks. Objectivity and responsibility, patience, endurance and self-discipline!
>
> (Wigman 1983a: 304)

CLASS AT THE MARY WIGMAN SCHOOL

When Ellen von Frankenberg took her first class at the Mary Wigman School in Dresden, the year was 1923. The school had been growing steadily during its initial two years and Wigman had gathered around her a fine group of teachers that included her sister Elisabeth, Berthe Trümpy and Hanya Holm. In the students' dressing room, an assortment of languages could be heard: English, Norwegian and Swedish, along with French and German. As the school grew a new studio space was renovated into the celebrated "yellow room" in which students took class and Wigman's first professional group rehearsed (Bell-Kanner 1991: 7–8).

As a beginning dancer, von Frankenberg had a clear recall of her own audition class, taught by Trümpy: the pianist played four-measure phrases while the class, with arms outstretched, began to circle the imaginary center of the room (ibid.: 9). Greater emphasis was placed on working with the group and adding to the communal expression and experience, instead of a display of technical prowess or of prior dance training. Accepted into the school as a beginner, von Frankenberg described the hierarchy of classes. Two classes were offered for the beginners, who were initiated by Elisabeth Wiegmann into fundamentals based on Mary's early work with Laban. His movement scales were taught just as tone scales are taught to a beginning pianist. But instead of following an aural key and pitch, the movement scales were intended to connect dimensional planes and activate the entire body and the space within and around the dancer. Trümpy and Holm alternated teaching the two more advanced classes wherein the fundamental concepts were developed and explored in depth. Finally, there was a master-level class that included the Wigman Group dancers. The teachers decided among themselves when a student was ready to advance to the next level of study (ibid.).

Mary Wigman was physically absent from the building much of the time, as the school's expenses made her touring a necessity throughout the 1920s and 1930s. Her professional aspirations as a concert performer remained strong, and the reputation of the school rested on her performance career and larger public persona. Von Frankenberg recalled that even while she was away, the impact of Wigman's personality was ever present. When she returned she would give some classes, watch student compositions and disappear again, leaving the students inspired with the sense that they'd taken part in an event of great magnitude. Von Frankenberg felt that Wigman was very conscious of the effect that her "rousing presence" had on the student dancers.

Study at the Mary Wigman School encompassed much more than studio classes. Students were constantly sent out to museums and encouraged to consider all aspects and mediums of art. Philosophy and history were part of study as the education of the mind traveled alongside the practice of the body. Von Frankenberg wrote that "In Mary's classes one really absorbed the meaning of modern art" (ibid.: 13). The emphasis was on exploration and students were expected to take responsibility for their own education in the larger world of aesthetics. So the school became a place of discovery and a meeting place for young people and new ideas. Rather than a studio solely for physical training, the goal was to educate the whole dancer in dance history, theory, composition and musical accompaniment, while making the body an articulate instrument of expression.

When you imagine Wigman's bright studio filled with dancers streaming barefoot in lines across the wooden floor or circling an unmarked but imaginatively potent center, where do you envision the mirror on the wall? A mainstay in most dance studios, the mirror – that blessing and curse of the dancer's day – was absent in the Wigman School. The goal of class was to experience the movement from the inside out rather than to impose an external ideal of placement or position on the body. Brigitta Herrmann, who studied at the Berlin Wigman School in the 1950s and 1960s, explains: "*We* were the mirrors" (Herrmann interview, Santa Fe, NM: 14 March 2006). Herrmann's experiences offer an exceptional view of Wigman's training methods at that period of her long teaching life. Having studied at the Palucca School in Leipzig from the age of sixteen, Herrmann had trained in classical Russian ballet as well as in Palucca's modern style, following the Palucca school curriculum. In contrast, class at the Wigman School was a revelation and an opening to the many levels of creative involvement in the study of *Ausdruckstanz*. While Herrmann went on to a long professional life in dance and theater, she saw that Wigman did not intend for all of her students to become professional dancers. In *ekstasis*, the ecstatic experience, Wigman felt that the dancer could come into the deepest state of performance. She worked to develop a way of dance study that could enable such experiences for her students, although all might not achieve them. What Wigman training did not do was definitively sculpt the dancing body into an ideal "professional" form as did ballet training or the codified technique of Martha Graham. Sandy Broyard studied at the Martha Graham School in New York and at the Berlin Wigman School in 1961. Her memories of Wigman are filled with an appreciation of Wigman's teaching style and for the gentleness with which Wigman treated those around her. On Sundays Wigman would invite her foreign students, who were far from home, to her own house where she made tea for them. Broyard was well aware that this sort of graciousness would never have occurred during her study with Graham in New York. She also recalls that the students gathered in Wigman's classes represented a broad range of experience, from professionals like Herrmann to farm girls taking their first dance classes. Bill Costanza was an American GI stationed in Germany in 1960. Remarkably, he received permission to attend Wigman's summer course, traveling through the Russian zone by train to dance. His memories of Wigman reveal an enduring fondness for her as a woman and as a teacher. He recalls his concern at first seeing Wigman teaching in her 70s, her frail figure moving forcefully yet precariously through the lines of dancers and "some were big girls" (Costanza interview, Martha's Vineyard, MA: 4 August 2007). Such a wide range of students were brought together in Wigman's classes and each was asked to develop an individual way of fulfilling the movement, whether the hour-long class was devoted to turning or to Wigman's signature vibration practice. Wigman recognized and encouraged them all. The goal was an enrichment of the whole person, physically and emotionally, through the practice of dance movement. And it is no wonder that, in some ways, Wigman's training methods are better recognized among movement therapists than in the world of concert dance.

Study with Wigman followed a definite structure. Classes were organized in hour-long blocks and the day started with stretching and warm-ups taught by Til Tiehle or Manja Chmiel. Once the muscles in the body were warm, the *Ubungstunde* or Training Hour began. A closer look at the structure of these training hour classes provides a view of what Wigman deemed the most important elements of the dance. Each training hour had as a theme a particular movement quality, such as walking, swinging or jumping. Throughout the hour, that movement would be developed, varied and embellished in much the same fashion that Wigman describes the process of composing a dance. The movement quality was introduced in a simple form. The movements were taken traveling across the floor, with the most advanced dancers in the lead. Line after line would cross the floor to return and begin again. Learning was done more through repetition than explanation, with the goal of experiencing the "feeling" of the movement. As the class progressed, levels of complexity were added to the basic movement quality. The German language famously combines words to expand the lexicon and allow a multitude of shaded meanings. In much the same way, Wigman's training hour offered traveling movement combinations that would build on each previous passage so students could assimilate the fundamental movement at the same time that they glimpsed limitless possibilities within that movement. Using repetition in this way and filling the class time with non-stop progressions demanded stamina and concentration. When it gets tired enough, the body releases and finds a new sensation that can become an epiphany. American dancer Alwin Nikolais describes an entire class period that Hanya Holm spent teaching arm swings. After that sort of experience, he said, one never looks at the movement in the same way again. Holm had carried this type of training from Wigman to students in the United States.

What were the movement qualities that Wigman selected to form the foundation for her dance? The following terms offer a glimpse into the basic building blocks of Mary Wigman's *Ausdruckstanz*:

Gehen (walking)
Gleiten (gliding)
Schreiten (to strike or stalk)
Fallen (falling, collapsing)
Stampfen (rhythm in the feet)
Ostinato (counter rhythm)

Vibrato (vibration)
Schweben (floating)
Schwingen (swinging)
Huepfen (skipping)
Springen (jumping)
Kreise (walking the circle)
Kreise ohne Fronveränderung (circling while changing facings)
Drehen (turning, spinning)
Gewichtverlagerung (shifting weight into running) then
Auffangen (catch and collapse)

DISCOVERING THE ELOQUENT BODY

In her desire to develop a technique most able to articulate the new language of dance, Wigman saw the work of a dancer as encompassing two large areas of practice: the first was a systematic study of expression as the retrieval and transformation of subconscious impulses that brought spiritual emotion into conscious physicality. Simultaneously, she recognized the need to develop what she termed the function of the dancer by physically training the body as an articulate instrument that portrayed these metaphysical states.

Mary Wigman was committed to the idea that dance training should serve the purpose of freeing the dancer in a process of individual discovery. She never codified her technique but she did provide clear structure for these explorations in her classes. She was adamant that she was not interested in making "little Mary Wigmans." For Wigman the goal of dance training was the development of the body as a versatile, communicating and very personal instrument. She did see that the development of a dancer proceeded in three states:

First stage: Wigman saw this stage growing solely from a desire for expression. This desire was not yet guided by content or form. Instead it was driven by expression for its own sake. She identifies "Dullness, chaos, unrestraint, agitation and rapture about the [new] awareness of body" (Wigman 1973: 127). Thus the individual could have a rapturous experience but one that lacked conscious awareness. To move toward consciousness, the dancer must enter the second stage.

Second stage: Wigman described this as the awakening of sense orientation. It is the point where the dancer struggles to grasp the formal elements that will eventually allow a conscious expression. The second stage is characterized by an internal discord, "the oscillation between expression for the sake of expression and form for the sake of form [as] the body, no longer mere corpus and not yet instrument, becomes the scene of inner and outer struggles" (ibid.). This is essential if the dancer's talent is to progress.

Third stage: in this stage, Wigman saw that a real understanding emerges. Expression and function are brought together. "The body, no longer willful substance, reveals itself as the tool for a purpose ..." (ibid.: 128).

This progression of a dancer's development makes possible, "the dancer's fitness for professional effectiveness" (ibid.). And it is important to understand that while many would benefit from a dance experience, the training of a professional dancer was focused and arduous, although it followed a very different course than that of ballet. For Wigman, emoting was not enough. This has been a common misunderstanding of her methodology since the time of her early fame up to the present. Wigman outlined the process of becoming a dancer, starting from the point of purely physical training, through thematic exploration, to the transcendent performance experience for the individual and finally for the individual within the group.

With that in mind, this section of exercises is intended to introduce two branches of the dance art as Wigman envisioned it: the outer/physical and the inner/emotional. While it is useful to identify a dichotomy of physical and emotional training, it is also important to remember that the two became inextricably intertwined in Wigman's practice and in the professional dancer. In class with Wigman, line after line of dancers would progress across the floor, sometimes in unison, sometimes in canon. Variation would be layered upon variation and the continuous energy of moving bodies would drive the class forward. While all of these movement qualities ideally could be explored in such a setting, these exercises can be modified to fit nearly any space or population as a simple introduction to Wigman's movement fundamentals.

WIGMAN MOVEMENT QUALITIES IN PRACTICE

GEHEN – WALKING

The simple act of placing the bare foot on the floor was of a great significance to Mary Wigman. Barefoot dancing represented a radical departure from the ballet, at once a return to a kind of earthiness and a cause of some scandal. Kay Bardsley recalls that when she took classes with Maria Theresa Duncan in a Greek settlement house in New York, many parents were outraged that their children would be dancing in such a "peasant" style with bare feet. The bare foot became the symbol of dance modernism, from Isadora Duncan through St. Denis, Graham, Humphrey, Wigman and those who followed. The feet presented a non-uniform of the modern dance as an emphatic connection to the earth and, most importantly, a new instrument capable of eloquent expression. Wigman wrote of the feet:

> The dancer's feet love the ground. Like small, tamed animals they slink across the floor with repressed wickedness, holding back their power to jump. They stroke the floor, grasp it with their toes, press against it, whispering their secrets.
>
> (Wigman 1973: 118)

Walking and running have become mainstays of postmodern dance choreography. The walk for Wigman was not pedestrian; it demanded a palette of steps, like a spectrum of colors that could represent the variety of human locomotion, literally and metaphorically. The walk could be a slow saunter, a swaying stroll, a deliberate striding or an angry storming. The range of what could be expressed simply through walking was vast. The articulation through the foot from heel to toe or toe to heel offered a multiplicity of ways to relate to the ground and thus to pass through the space. Walks could drive the energy downward into the earth or lift the dancer up, resisting the pull of gravity. They could be done with the whole foot or only on the ball of the foot. A walk could be taken directly forward or backward or on the diagonal with the body in profile. The diagonal walk, especially, offered a manifestation of the oppositional tension, the push and pull of opposing forces. Most importantly, Wigman emphasized the experience of walking itself. Most of us walk every day, yet the goal of the walking practice was to bring the walker into the present moment and to demand concentrated attention to a sensation that had become automatic. It also served to settle the dancer in preparation for more complex activities. Practiced before performance, the simple exercise of walking and feeling the feet in contact with the floor can literally ground the performer before she goes onstage.

EXERCISE 4.1: TAKING THE FEET FOR A WALK

▶ Let's start with the simple and important practice of walking. Start by feeling the soles of your feet against the floor. Is the surface warm or cool, rough or smooth? Begin walking with your regular walk. Keep all your attention on your feet. How does your foot move to allow you to walk? Do you roll through from heel to toe, foot flat or toe first? Try each of these ways of walking. Read again Wigman's description of the feet. Can you stroke the floor with your feet in place? Traveling? How does the stroke change as you begin to move through the space? How can you strike the floor? Or stalk from corner to corner? Can you grasp the floor with your toes? Press against the floor to rise. How does walking on the balls of your feet change your whole body's relationship to the floor? Try Wigman's image of the feet as "small tamed animals." Can the feet "slink across the floor with repressed wickedness?" What does repressed wickedness look like when expressed with the foot alone? What other images can you think of to inspire the feet? Can feet be sneaky or bold, quiet or loud? What happens when you speed your walk to a run?

GLEITEN – GLIDING

Gliding is a very specific variation on the theme of walking. In gliding the feet are flat and slide across the surface of the floor. Nothing should disturb the smoothness of the movement. Of course there is some lift allowed, otherwise you couldn't travel at all! But rather than coming from articulation through the foot, ankle and then lifting of the knee, gliding comes from the entire leg, reaching from the hip. There is a conscious effort to lengthen the space between the legs, as in a shallow forward lunge. In gliding the level of the body remains constant. It is as if you are on a conveyor belt traveling on a steady stream of motion. When you are gliding forward, the sternum or breastbone will naturally take the lead. In backward gliding, the small of the back takes the lead, with the abdominal muscles engaged in a small contraction. Clearly, gliding can easily travel forward and backward. Gliding through space can be direct and linear. But gliding is especially suited to carving curves through the space. Just as the gliding proceeds in a smooth, ongoing progression, so do curvilinear lines link as a chain, one to another. Gliding is continuous.

> She slowly strides across the floor and closes her eyes. She no longer feels anything but the rhythm of striding ... The floor responds, returns every

pressure, instinctively offering embrace with motherly love. Every step is a caress, a touch of tenderness.

(Wigman 1973: 118)

EXERCISE 4.2: GLIDING THROUGH SPACE

▶ Start with knees softly bent and the feet in conscious contact with the surface of the floor. Bend your arms at right angles in front of you with palms facing toward the floor. With your arms in this position, lift your shoulders toward your ears, then let your scapulae slide smoothly down your back as you lower your shoulders to a neutral position. Begin to move smoothly forward, finding evenness in the rhythm, length and level of your glide. Try it backwards. Release your arms to your sides but keep them falling from the shoulders and actively maintaining their relationship to the torso. Then travel with a curving pathway, beginning with a large curve across the floor. Starting from upstage right, glide in a single arc that takes you toward downstage center and continues to move you to a point of arrival at upstage left. Reverse the pathway while gliding backwards. Choose a smaller curvilinear path that carves small arcs. Connect the arcs into a scalloping pattern with three, four or five glides forward and a half turn to travel three gliding steps backwards and repeat the pattern. How does the upper body respond to the curving path of the gliding feet? There are many variations possible when gliding. Consider the varied pathways that the gliding body can take through the space.

STAMPFEN – RHYTHM IN THE FEET

We've read of Wigman's demand that innate body rhythm initiate the pulse of the dance. While rhythm can occur in any part of the body, the feet are especially suited for exploring the rhythms of dance. Gliding offers a way to experience a smooth and sustained sense of time, but the feet can create the opposite effect.

Sometimes the dancing feet turn wild: then they rage against the mother in angry rhythms, stamping furiously against the floor, threatening utter ruin. Untouched by their hatred, the ground goes on breathing deeply and quietly. The frantic feet stop, astonished, confused, stretching themselves arrogantly at their ankles, turning laughingly on their toes. Yes, they can be frivolous too.

(Wigman 1973: 118)

EXERCISE 4.3: WILD FEET

▶ Have one person clap a rhythm. Have the other dancers respond by clapping the same rhythm in unison. Do this several times with different "clappers" setting the rhythms. Next have one person clap a rhythm while the group responds by repeating the rhythm with their feet. Then have one dancer stamp a rhythm while the other dancers begin to move to that rhythm through space. From that rhythm, develop your own variation. Vary the time and intensity of the beats: sometimes fast or slow, soft or emphatic. Read again Wigman's description of when the dancing feet turn wild. Can they rage against the floor? Can they stop in confusion and then become frivolous? What sort of rhythm would frivolous feet make? Could you take that rhythm into your hands and clap it? Could you take any of these rhythms into another body part?

OSTINATO – DIFFERENT RHYTHMS IN FEET AND ARMS

Ostinato is a term that Wigman adapted from music theory. In ostinato a phrase is repeated insistently in the bass line throughout a composition while the upper, treble parts change. Musical fundamentals like ostinato directed the experiments that Emile Jaques-Dalcroze presented to his students at Hellerau. Mary Wigman imported the term "ostinato" to the dancing form and used it to signify the use of counter rhythms between parts of the body, for example between the feet and the arms.

EXERCISE 4.4: OSTINATO

▶ Listen to Chopin's *Fantaisie-Impromptu* for piano. Can you discern the square structure of four sixteenth notes in the right hand against the swing of triplets in the left hand in each measure? Can you put these rhythms in your own body? Try the following exercise.

▶ Establish a rhythmic pattern in one area of your body – try your feet. Keep it in 4/4 time to begin with (count and step 1, 2, 3, 4). Practice this pattern until you can comfortably repeat it. Then establish another rhythmic pattern in another body area – say your arms. Keep this rhythm in 3/4 time (count 1, 2, 3). Practice this pattern until you can comfortably repeat it. Now go back to the rhythm in your feet. Keep it going and add the arm pattern. Trade rhythms between upper and lower body parts. Try new rhythms. Try them with different body parts.

VIBRATO – VIBRATION

Vibrato is another idea from music vocabulary, wherein expressive quality is given to the sound of a note by means of rapid and minute fluctuations in pitch. Translating the idea for dance, Wigman's vibrations were achieved through a buoyant vertical bounce of the body, sometimes slight and at times more vigorous, either with the whole body or with a single body part. The vibration usually was done traveling across the floor, with many variations, from a light, lifted vibration on the balls of the feet to a deeper bounce with the whole foot placed firmly against the floor. The vibration was achieved through a release in the ankles and a resilience in the knees and hips that was supported by a resonating, lightly panting breath. The hands sometimes rested on the ribcage in order to bring awareness to the breath.

Wigman developed the quality of vibration after an injury curtailed her own ability to jump. The up-and-down motion of the vibration is like a very small lifting and landing that reaches into the heart of jumping.

At the Wigman School, students were encouraged to explore for themselves and to solve the problems presented by the movement qualities. Hanya Holm describes how she and a group of students came to understand the vibration:

> We found the answer to it while sitting on a sofa a whole night, with the springs helping us to bounce back. Then, on our feet without any outward help, the demands of the momentum carried us gradually further until the repetition of the movement finally broke down any mental opposition, and vibration became a true experience for us.
>
> (Holm in Sorell 1969: 18)

EXERCISE 4.5: VIBRATIONS

▶ Bounce on something with springs: a couch or bed or hammock. Try this sitting or standing (carefully!) Try it with eyes open and eyes closed. Try to focus on the changes in level and the moment of change from up to down and vice versa. Then see those changes as part of a continuum. Mary Wigman's practice of the vibration was very specific and thus difficult to recreate without a knowing presence in the studio. However, the concept can be explored as an idea of a movement type. A very fine example of the vibrations can be seen in the video, *Hanya: Portrait of a Pioneer*, where Hanya Holm leads a group of students in vibration practice outdoors at Mills College in the 1930s.

SCHWINGEN – SWINGING

For Mary Wigman the movement of the swing could be the basis of an entire dance composition as well as a singular physical activity or a formal element in a larger choreographic work. She describes swing dances as arising from the pure joy or pleasure of moving. "These are based on the swing of the body and its extension in sweeping through space as curve. Their nature has an externally flowing quality. They are less bound by metrics than by space" (Wigman 1973: 92).

EXERCISE 4.6: SWINGING

▶ Make sure that you have plenty of space around you. Raise one arm high overhead and allow it to drop forward and back, falling from the shoulder. Reverse the swing from back to front. Experiment by swinging the arm from side to side across the body and on the diagonal. Stick with one swinging motion for several minutes or longer. Close your eyes. Imagine the experience of a child riding a swing. Envision the suspension, the fall and the catch of the forward and backward movement. Allow your body to experience the swing through your imagination, while standing still. Now reach both arms upward and swing through the whole body from front to back and then back to front, releasing through the hip, knee and ankle joints with the down swing. Try swinging with the leg alone releasing at the hip. The range of a swing is directly related to effort of the suspending reach and the releasing joints. *Anspannung* and *Abspannung* are integral to the swing. Doris Humphrey's fall and recovery has made the swing a staple in American modern dance. In class with Wigman, exploring the action of the swing could fill an entire class period, building from a localized swinging arm to a full-bodied sweeping through space propelled by the momentum of the swing. Many, many variations of the swing can be seen in dance classes. Find a swing in playground, park or schoolyard. Reacquaint yourself with the sensation of swinging.

HUEPFEN – SKIPPING (THIS MAY ALSO GO ALONG WITH SWINGING)

EXERCISE 4.7: SKIPPING

▶ Start with a simple skip across the floor, alternating the feet and allowing your arms to travel naturally at your sides. Increase your effort so that your skips become more energized, pressing the right knee forward as you push off from the floor with your left foot and vice versa. Bring the arms into action, one swinging forward and one back in opposition to the skipping legs. Skip with the intention of really wanting to get somewhere. Try it with both arms swinging forward and both back or opening to the sides and closing with the alternating swings. Add the upper body and head. How can they respond to the skips and be part of the swings? What variations can you discover?

KREISE – WALKING A CIRCLE

Kreise ohne Frontveränderung – circling with facings.

For Wigman, the circle had great import, just as it has been recognized as the core of traditional folk dances from around the world. More than a geometric shape, for Wigman the circle was a cosmic concept, and in her exercises incorporated multiple explorations of the idea of the circle.

> Her body draws a circle into space, the feet move with wide, intense steps around the circle's line, and, in moving, always hit upon the same points of the circle. She holds sway over the circle in space while being held by it.
>
> (Wigman 1973: 120)

DREHEN – TURNING AND SPINNING

The yin–yang symbol that greeted those entering the *Festhalle* at Hellerau became a symbol of deep resonance for Wigman as she developed her dance technique. And Laban had shared with her his experience of the mystical dancing prayer of the Sufi dervishes. The vertical center of the yin–yang represents the mystic "center," where there is no rotation, no restlessness, no impulse, nor any suffering of any kind. It is the "still point of the turning world", as T.S. Eliot described it in *Burnt Norton*. These philosophical ideas run throughout

Mary Wigman's writings about turning and the circle. And training to turn and spin was central to her pedagogy over the span of her teaching life. They also formed the theme of her 1926 solo *Drehentanz*, or *Monotonie Whirl*, in which she spun for seven minutes without stopping. In Wigman's treatment of the turning body we see most clearly her wedding of the individual dancer to the space surrounding her.

> A secret power emanates from this circle and directs the feet ... Indeed, a living circle this dancer is, subject to the very law conjured up by herself!
> Suddenly – an idea striking like lightning; the center. To become the center herself, and then from there to destroy the self-created madness!
>
> (ibid.)

Hanya Holm wrote of the struggle among Wigman's students to master spinning for an extended period of time. Many were left clinging to the walls to find equilibrium and others were sent flying down the hall with nausea. But when captured, spinning is one of the most compelling of Wigman's elements to practice and mesmerizing to behold. The video *Mary Wigman: When the Fire Dances Between the Two Poles* has a sequence in which Wigman teaches a spinning class in her Berlin studio and illustrates the spin in practice. When watching the sequence, play close attention to the placement of the feet and the response of the upper body to them. As with the vibrations, Mary Wigman's practice of spinning was very specific and thus difficult to recreate without an experienced teacher in the studio. However, the concepts of circling, turning and spinning can be explored as an idea of a movement type and a practice of the body's relationship to the space around it. Wigman knew well the power of the circle as physical property and cosmic metaphor.

EXERCISE 4.8: CIRCLING, TURNING AND SPINNING

(1) Drawing the circle

▶ Begin standing with the feet parallel, with the knees bent in a *demi plié*. Bearing weight on the left foot, straighten the left leg while reaching the right leg forward, side and back to close again in parallel *plié*. Repeat on the left side. Try it again and envision that you are drawing an arc on the floor to the right and to the left. Both arcs have the parallel *plié* as their point of returning to center. For experienced dancers, this is a parallel *rond de jamb*. Now add a simultaneous reach of the arm, creating a parallel arc at torso height, as you circle the leg: forward, side and back. Reverse the pathway from back to front. Try it with a six-count circling: reaching 1, 2, 3, 4, 5 and *plié* together on 6. **Establish a sequence**: Right leg and arm front to back, left leg and arm front to back, then right side back to front and left side back to front. Repeat.

(2) Walking the circle

▶ Begin with the right foot, walking an imaginary circle through the space to your right. Try taking five steps: right, left, right, left, right and shift your direction at count six on the right foot to begin to walk the arc toward the left. Repeat the five steps in the left arc: left, right, left, right, left and shift to the right again. Essentially, you are walking a horizontal figure eight with the shift as the center point that changes directions. Try tilting the body toward the direction of the turn. Find the centripetal force that draws the torso toward the center. Visualize the center of each circle. Stretch your arms out sideways at shoulder height. As you walk and tilt your body, allow your arms to establish the center point. Thus your right hand reaches toward the center of the circle to the right and your left hand does the same in the left circle. **Establish a sequence**: Starting with the right foot, walk the circle to the right and shift, walk the circle to the left and shift. Repeat the circles and add the body tilt. Repeat the circles again and add the arms. You can also establish a rhythm: Five counts to the right, shift on six and five counts to the left and shift.

(3) Circling while facing front

▶ Consider the circles that you have traced through space in your figure eights.
▶ Now begin to walk a new circle while maintaining your facing toward the front. Imagine yourself standing still at the center. Picture the face of a clock. Straight before you is twelve o'clock. Directly to your right is three o'clock. Behind you lies six o'clock and nine o'clock is to your left.
▶ Keep your shoulders and pelvis facing directly to the front of the room throughout your walking. Step your right foot forward toward the right at two o'clock. Step your left foot across and behind at four o'clock. Bring the right foot behind the left at six o'clock. Take the left foot open to the left at eight o'clock. Bring the right foot across and forward of the left at ten o'clock. Bring the left foot forward to twelve o'clock. Thus, in six steps you have traversed the edges of a circle while keeping a single focus, in this case forward.

▶ Try walking the circle while facing front again; keep the knees soft and the legs slightly turned out to facilitate the sideways motion. Allow your pace to build gradually as you grow comfortable with the pattern of the feet. Find a pace and placement of the feet that allows your steps to become smooth and even. Now begin to allow the rest of your body to respond to the circular pathway as if the whole body was moving inside a large cylinder. Again, maintain a forward focus through the shoulders and pelvis even as you step to the side. Imagine your torso contacting the circle in space through your right side, back, left side and front and all of the subtle places between these points. Allow your head to respond to the shifts in your body. Place your fingertips at your shoulders with the elbows opened wide to the sides. Repeat.

▶ **Establish a sequence**: Beginning with the right foot, circle in six steps while facing front and repeat, then add the torso, repeating the circle two times. Finally, bring the fingertips to the shoulders and circle twice more. Thus the sequence builds from feet, to feet and torso, to feet, torso and arms. You can establish a rhythm by taking six counts for every time around, thus the above sequence would have six repetitions of six counts. Now try the whole thing on the left side!

▶ It is possible to change facings by turning the entire body a quarter or a half turn at the beginning of every new repetition. It is easiest to turn toward the right side when stepping out with the right foot and toward the left side when stepping with the left.

▶ It is also possible to **create a longer phrase** by joining all of the circling and turning sequences above. For example: Combine one full sequence of **(1) drawing the circle** from right to left, then add one full sequence of **(2) walking the circle** from right to left and continue by squaring the body to the front and adding one full sequence of **(3) circling while facing front** on both the right and left sides. The entire phrase can be done in 3/4 time counting 1, 2, 3, 4, 5, 6.

▶ The variations in such turning phrases are many. In the phrase above, the emphasis is placed on first establishing the dancer at the center of a larger circle through drawing the circle around a stationary body. By walking two con-joined circles, the body is moved to the periphery or the outline of the circle in space. By circling while facing front, the entire body fills the volume of the circle. The final step would be to draw the energy of the circle form to the very center of the dancing body through spinning practice. Thus the dancer equally shapes, is moved by and becomes one with the cosmic force of the circle.

SPRINGEN – JUMPING

Every leap is a battle between the upward drive toward weightlessness and the somber reality of the earthbound being. When jumps were the theme of the training hour, the entire class was spent on jumping. No small challenge for the students that day! The jumps started small. Building to the two-footed take-off and landing of a true jump, the air was filled with hops that grew to skips that progressed to leaps. The breath was integral to the success of the jump. The legs remained buoyant throughout, pressing against the ground to spring and yielding into the floor on landing. Inhalation offered a key to buoyancy. At the peak of the jump the inhalation was sustained for just a moment, to keep the body airborne for as long as possible. In the leap we see full exertion of the muscles and limbs with the support of the inner breath.

> She jumps because she wants to fly, battling during the leap with gravity and lightness, overcoming the one to be conquered by the other.
>
> (Wigman 1973: 119)

EXERCISE 4.9: JUMPING AND BREATH

▶ Endless variations are possible on the theme of jumping, from the airbound leap that evolves from a run, to the vertical jump when both feet leave the floor simultaneously. The form of the jump depends on the expertise of the dancer, but all jumping begins with a *plié* or bending of the leg that connects the body to the earth, and continues through the press and spring upward that culminates in the landing *plié*, allowing the body to yield again to earthly contact. Whether you are comfortable with a bounding leap across the floor, a jump in place or any variation, try adding an inhalation through the takeoff and the high point of your jump. See how the breath can support the suspension of the body in space. This use of breath can be consciously incorporated into any jumping practice.

Mary Wigman also used a very specific kind of jump when making her "grotesque" dances such as the *Hexentanz* or the Dance of the Demon in *The Seven Dances of Life*. In these dances, the leaps and jumps are consciously earthbound. The legs pull in toward the body and the pull of gravity downward remains strong. It can be useful to think of this sort of elevation as a jump done in a box where there is a ceiling or a point where the upward momentum is arrested and drawn into the body center. Try your earlier flying jumps and leaps, this time keeping a lid on the high level. How does this change the feeling and shape of the jump? How does it change the expression transmitted to those watching? When would this sort of jump be useful in a choreographed work?

FALLEN – FALLING, COLLAPSING

GEWICHTVERLAGERUNG – SHIFTING OF WEIGHT INTO RUNNING, AND *AUFFANGEN* – CATCH AND COLLAPSE

Perhaps no other act represents *Abspannung* and *Anspannung* more than falling: the absolute release of the body to gravity, the suspension that precedes it and the gathering of forces that allows a rise and a repetition of the entire sequence. Falling practice for Wigman, while allowing for endless variations, grew from a very specific sequence. First there was a conscious shifting of the weight into a running through space that was caught, arrested. And from this suspension of momentum, really an in-breath of intention, the whole body surrendered to the downward pull. The fall could happen slowly or quickly, but always with a conscious control.

EXERCISE 4.10: FALLING

▶ Experiment with ways of falling. Begin with a run leading to a suspension and collapse as described above. Listen to your muscles. How much tension and how much release is required to smoothly execute a slow collapse or a quick one? Listen to your bones. How must the joints respond so as to support a smooth descent and an equally fluid rising? Listen to your breath. How can your breath assist with your falling?

At the Wigman School, a full class period was dedicated to each of the above movement qualities on a rotating basis. The very nature of the training hour promoted the possibility of an uplifting experience. Analysis happened on the fly and the whole structure of the class was aimed at an increasing level of muscular involvement and excitement, with the goal of "being danced" or carried along by the flow of the movement and the energy of the group moving together. Progressing from the simplest version to the most complex, each exercise was mined for its full range of possibilities and, rather than attaining an ideal form of the walk or the jump, the swing or the fall, the class was shaped to allow the movement to develop through intensive practice and repetition with the hope of a conscious total experience.

WHAT MAKES THE DANCE?

In *The Mary Wigman Book*, Wigman lays bare her goals for training the body. All were intended to fulfill the range of human expression in dance form. She saw this training as the first step to finding the power of the body as an instrument for the outward manifestation of changes in our invisible emotional states. She called this physicality "function" and divided the dancing functions among parts of the body. Reminiscent of **Delsarte**'s divisions of the body, the primary dancing functions were defined as:

1. Tension – the function of the muscles.
2. Rhythm – the function of the limbs.
3. Breathing – the function of the vital organs (Wigman 1973: 88).

François Delsarte (1811–71) – developed a system of "harmonic body movements" and *tableau vivant*. Delsarte's theory divided the human body into three distinct zones: the head and upper chest as the spiritual center; the torso as the seat of emotions; and the abdomen and pelvis as the physical center. Delsarte's ideas formed the basis for many philosophical and theatrical principles.

In Wigman's *Ausdruckstanz*, each part of the body became an eloquent member of the whole. Expression was not limited to the center or core or the limbs. Each body part must be awakened in order to contribute to the complete form of the dance. The following exercises offer an opportunity to explore these functions and bring to life Wigman's concepts of the essential elements of dance, including breath, space, time and effort/strength.

EXERCISE 4.11: SEQUENTIAL STRETCHES

▶ Find a place on the floor. Lie down. Release your body into the floor. Feel the surface of the floor against your body. Feel the air around you and how it plays on the surface of your skin. Close your eyes. And begin to listen to your breathing. Pay attention to the changes that happen in your torso as you breathe in and out. Do you take more time to inhale or exhale? Is your breathing regular or varied? Is there a pattern to your breath? As you turn your focus inward, try to relax your muscles more and more with each exhalation. As the muscles loosen, feel your body soften into the floor.

▶ Then turn your focus to your fingertips. See what small movements you can make with the tips of your fingers. Can you move each fingertip, one at a time? How do they want to move together? Begin to make the movement of your fingertips larger, using the whole finger. How does that affect the movement of your hand? Become aware of the palm of your hand. How does closing the fingers inward change the palm and the back of the hand? And how does stretching the fingers change them? How do these larger movements of the fingers and hand affect the wrist? As you begin to move the fingertips, fingers, hands and wrists, notice how the muscles in your forearms respond. And what does moving these muscles do to your elbows?

▶ Allow the elbows to join in the dance of fingertips, fingers, hands, wrists and forearms. What sorts of movement do the elbows allow? And how does this movement affect the upper arms, the biceps and triceps? How does movement from the fingertips through the arms resonate in the shoulders?

▶ What sort of message can travel from the fingers to the shoulder joint? How many ways can the shoulder joints move? As you make your movements larger, see if you can find how the shoulder joint changes the bones and muscles of the upper back and chest. Take a moment and feel this dance of fingers, hands, wrists, forearms, elbows, upper arm and shoulder in every direction around your prone form. How does your neck respond? And your head? Imagine how this movement would change the focus of your gaze if your eyes were open. Allow the center of the body to become involved. Twist or stretch at the waist and feel how your abdominal and back muscles support your movement.

▶ In this upper body dance, inhale and stretch from the center of the torso to the fingertips. Exhale and release the stretch. Do this several times, ending with a release back into the floor. In the final release, make the body still and begin to listen to your breathing again.

▶ Now take the focus to your toes. How articulate can you be with the tips of your toes? Can you move each toe in isolation? Can you move them sequentially? Expand your toes by stretching and draw them in by grasping. How do these movements affect the soles of your feet? Draw circles in the air with your toes, or triangles or octagons. Write your name. Try your first name with your left foot and your last name with your right foot. How does moving your foot affect your ankle? And how does ankle movement change the muscles in your shins and calves? Point and flex. How does pointing change your calf muscles and flexing change those of your shin?

▶ Allow the movement impulse from toe to foot to ankle to lower leg to continue to your knee joints. What sort of movements do the knees make possible? And how do the thighs respond to this movement? When you take the movement into the thighs, what happens in the hip joints? What sort of message can travel from the toes to the hip joints? And from the hips to the toes? What sort of movements do the hip joints make possible? How does your pelvis respond? And your abdominal and back muscles?

▶ In this lower body dance, inhale and stretch from the center of your pelvis to your toes. Exhale and release the stretch.

▶ Now connect the lower and upper body. Starting with fingertips and toes, let the movement grow to include hands and feet, wrists and ankles, forearms and lower legs, elbows and knees, upper arms and thighs, shoulders and hip joints. Feel the beautiful balance and correspondence between the muscles, bones and joints of the upper and lower body. And how do the torso and pelvis, spine, neck and head respond to this full-bodied movement? Now initiate the movement from the center, from the pelvis and inner torso out to the extremities.

EXERCISE 4.12: STRETCHING DANCE

▶ Remember Wigman's statement that the secret of the dance lies in "the living breath." Breath support for movement became an integral part of her performance and of how she taught dance. The expansion and contraction of the lungs serves as an automatic example of expansion and condensing within the body center.

▶ Take the sequential stretch from Exercise 4.11 into a full-bodied stretching dance. Feel the tension through the center as you reach right hand from left foot. Try the reverse. Stretch long, from fingertips to toes. As you stretch, begin to bring your attention back to your breath. As you inhale, stretch the body in any way you wish. As you exhale, allow the body to condense. Continue this breathing, stretching dance by expanding or opening on the inhalation and condensing or closing on the exhalation. Try different body parts and the whole body.

▶ Now reverse the breath/stretch pattern. Try stretching or expanding on the exhale and closing or condensing when you inhale. Does one pattern or the other feel most natural to your body? Spend some time in that pattern, then alternate between the two.

▶ Expand this stretching dance to rise. Eventually, come to standing and still-ness. Press your feet into the floor. Listen to your breath. Can you feel your heartbeat?

EXERCISE 4.13: BREATH PHRASE

▶ Take your stretching dance from Exercise 4.12 to the standing position. Your **kinesphere** is the space around you. As far as you can reach and in all directions, your kinesphere is your self-space. Find the edges of your kinesphere by stretching your limbs in front, behind, beside, above and below you. Imagine a large circle surrounding you and your body, poised within the sphere like Leonardo da Vinci's proportional drawings of Man.

▶ Once you have found the edges of your kinesphere, begin to use your breath to further explore what movements are possible in this space. As you did on the floor, expand with the inhalation and condense with the exhalation. Reverse this pattern by expanding with the out breath and closing with the in breath. Vary the breathing pattern, a quick breath out and a long, slow breath in. While riding your breath, begin to create a movement phrase that is completely dependent on your own breath pattern. This is the breath phrase.

Kinesphere – the reach space surrounding an individual, whose space consciousness is the awareness of their own place in space and the use of their kinesphere. The pathway is a prescribed or chosen path of a body through space.

EXERCISE 4.14: BREATHING THROUGH SPACE

▶ Begin walking quickly through the space. Notice how many steps it takes for you to fully inhale and how many steps it takes you to exhale. Imagine that your feet are like paint brushes: each step or glide or hop leaves a trace of color on the floor. With this in mind, travel along a straight or linear pathway, then try a curving or curvilinear path. Try varying your pathway between straight and curved. Add corresponding movements of the arms and upper body. Once again, use the breath to initiate and drive the movement. Now add the whole body breath phrase as you travel on your path.

SPACE

Wigman had used her time with Rudolph von Laban well. She was present for the early explorations that resulted in Laban's analysis of movement possibilities within the multi-dimensional space of the icosahedron. Wigman expanded on these theories from her experience as a consummate performer. Remember that for Wigman, space was the great, constant, invisible partner. While the space had mystical and metaphorical significance, it is important to remember that air does have actual weight. When Mary Wigman danced at Carnegie Hall, the space inherently contained 70,000 pounds of air! In many ways, Wigman's ideas were as closely bound to science as they were to aesthetics.

EXERCISE 4.15: SPACE AS INVISIBLE PARTNER

▶ Lie down comfortably on the floor with plenty of space around you. Take time to stretch your torso and limbs in whatever ways are most appropriate to your body in this place, at this time. Listen to the messages from your muscles and joints. This is your warm-up. Once stretched, allow your body to release totally into the floor. At the sound of the drum (or count) take twelve beats to rise to standing in any way you wish. Take ten beats to descend to the floor again. Take eight beats to rise and eight beats to descend. Try new ways of rising and descending. Repeat with four beats up and four beats down. Then in two beats each: up, down, up, down, and finish standing.

▶ Close your eyes to bring the focus inward. Begin to move a hand through the space around you. Imagine that the space is filled with champagne or soda. This effervescence allows your hand and arm to be buoyant and move freely and easily through the space. Reach with your fingers. Tickle the air.

▶ Now imagine that the champagne has turned to water and it is deep water, like that found at the deep end of a swimming pool. Feel the resistance of the water as you push, press and reach your arm through the space. How does your wrist respond? Your elbow?

▶ Now imagine that the water has turned to molasses. The space is filled with a viscous substance that creates more resistance as you move through this thicker space. How do your fingers, hand, arm and shoulder respond to this increasing pressure from the space itself? What must your muscles do to push your hand through the space?

▶ Finally, imagine that the space is filled with wet sand. How does this change the pressure and tension in your arm? How does the rest of your body, pelvis, thighs, chest and feet, respond to the space pressing in on you? What must you do to carve this heavy space? Could you take a few steps through this space? How does the resistance of the space shape your movement? How does it change your breathing?

▶ Now, while standing still, return to the sense of lightness in a space filled with champagne. Listen to your breath. Open your eyes. Take eight beats to descend to the floor as if the floor were pushing against you, resisting your descent. Take eight beats to rise as if the sky or ceiling were pressing you down, resisting your rising. Take four beats down with no resistance. Rise in four beats, resisting the rising. Descend in two beats with resistance. Rise in two beats with no resistance. Try single beats with resistance and without.

▶ Consider how your relationship with the space informed your movement. How can this relationship with space influence muscular tension and release, timing and intention?

▶ How can this experience prove useful in choreography and performance?

DANCE AS LANGUAGE

HANDS

From her earliest experience of seeing the Wiesenthal sisters in concert, Wigman had been aware of the expressive potential of the hands. In class, students were guided in explorations to animate the hands by using emotional cues. The imagery was vivid: hands that can cry, that can laugh happily and also express struggle, sadness and the gentleness of the dance. Consider the dance elements with which we have already experimented. Tension and release come into use when dancing with the hands. How does the idea of struggle affect the tension in your hands? What is the difference between a hand that laughs and a hand that cries? How does the speed with which you move your hands change as the emotion changes? And how do your hands move through space? Do you use the space close to you or far away to reach with longing or sadness? How do effort, space and time affect the dance of the hands?

EXERCISE 4.16: HAND DANCES

▶ Make a list of emotional qualities, for example, anger, fear, greed, lust, hope, longing, joy, tenderness, rage, sadness. And make a list of actions such as laughing, weeping, hiding, sneaking, struggling, yielding, caressing. Sitting in a circle, take your focus to your own hands. As a group, consider each of these emotional qualities and actions through improvisation, allowing yourself to explore this range of emotions through the hands alone. Begin to notice how these hand studies can affect the entire body. Repeat the hand explorations, but this time allow the entire body to respond. This can be done seated and taken to standing.

SPEAKING BEYOND THE INDIVIDUAL BODY

WORKING WITH OTHERS AND THE STRENGTH OF THE DANCING ENSEMBLE

These exercises can be for any number of dancers. Live accompaniment is preferred. They can be done solo, in unison with the entire group or divided into smaller groups with actors and observers.

EXERCISE 4.17: FINDING HOME

▶ In silence, find a place in the room that will be home for you right now. Go there and settle. Sit, stand and/or lie there. Inhabit that particular place and explore it. Close your eyes and imagine that your body is filling your home space. Stretch, relax or pace. Do anything that will allow you to connect with this place at this time. Finally, stretch out long, against the floor and feel where the surface of your body connects to the room. This can be a good time to practice the sequential stretches from Exercise 4.11. Finally, come to standing and bring your awareness to the sensation of the soles of your feet against the floor.

▶ At the sound of the drum, or piano or counting voice, begin to walk away from your dance home, out into open space. See the others moving through the room and become aware of the rhythm of your walk. Speed or slow the pace in response to changes in the sound accompaniment. When the sound stops, find a still shape and stay in place. Become aware of your home place. As if that spot were emitting a magnetic pull, begin to travel back home. It may not be in front of you, but rather beside or behind. Feel the pull on the part of your body closest to home as you initiate your return.

▶ A myriad of possibilities are available in finding and moving away from home. Explorations of pathways, tempo, stillness and emotion abound. The magnetic pull of points in space offers another way to experience surroundings as tangible with agency that affects the dancer. It is possible to leave home and return numerous times and in many ways. It is also possible to connect with another dancer when away from home.

EXERCISE 4.18: MIRRORING

▶ An old standby in improvisation and theater classes, the mirroring exercise initiates an immediate kinesthetic response between partners and a practical example of kinetic sympathy.

▶ Sit face to face and take your focus out over your partner's right shoulder. Choose one person to lead as the other partner mirrors the leader's movements. In mirroring, if the leader moves her right hand, the partner would move the left. The goal of mirroring is to transmit movement without speaking and to enliven the space between the two dancers. After a few minutes, change leaders and repeat. Finally, neither partner leads, but instead both respond and share the initiation of the movements without talking. This exercise, while simple, calls for complete attention to the movement and the interplay of forces between partners. Allow some time to discuss the mirroring experience. What was it like to lead? To be led? To share the leadership?

EXERCISE 4.19: DANCING CONVERSATIONS

▶ Return to facing your partner. Rather than experiencing movement simultaneously, a non-verbal conversation will take place between the partners. The movement conversation may be literal or very abstract. It may take the form of a narrative or a stream of consciousness, emphatic, dramatic and emotional, or matter-of-fact and understated. The challenge of the dancing conversation is to be still and "listen" before responding. One person starts the dancing conversation while the other watches and then responds through the body alone. The conversation continues back and forth between partners and can evolve to a standing conversation.

▶ It can be curious to observe how speaking styles translate to the dancing conversation. Some conversations never quite connect; some partners have trouble really listening and continue with their own dancing monologue. Some are impatient and "talk" over the other dancer who is still moving. Some dancers finish each other's sentences. Some are emphatic while others are subdued. It can be useful to have one couple continue while the others stop and watch.

EXERCISE 4.20: WALKING PARTNERS

▶ Standing side by side and shoulder to shoulder, partners gather at one side of the room. Looking straight ahead (and never into the mirror, nor with sly, sideways glances) the partners begin to travel across the floor. The goal is to move together to the other side of the room. The goal is not to trick one's partner, although that could be another exercise. While the partners may be most comfortable starting with walking forward, any variation is valid as long as both can travel together in shared movement.

▶ Choose one partner to begin as leader. Halfway across, without talking, change leaders. The moment when leadership changes is a crucial one and is similar to the sharing of the lead in the mirroring exercise. The space between the dancers is once again charged. How do bodies communicate with one another? What happens to timing and effort in this exercise? How can we use these ideas and awareness onstage and in life?

EXERCISE 4.21: THE GROUP IN SPACE

▶ Expanding on the practice of walking partners, join together two or more pairs of dancers. They may start standing, sitting, kneeling or each finding their own unique starting position. They should be quite close together, at least to begin. Let them be still until an impulse to move arises from someone in the group. Together, the group travels through space, not necessarily with the same movements as was the case for the walking partners exercise. Most importantly, the initial impulse to move and the dynamic quality of the movement is shared, as may be the impulse to stillness or urgency. It is possible to direct the focus of the group inward within itself or outward toward a fixed point or end goal. The idea of a magnetic pull through space can press the group toward a direction or destination or it can repel the group away from a particular location.

EXERCISE 4.22: CRYSTALLIZATION (BASED ON THE GROUP MOTION WORKSHOP)

▶ This exercise is for five to limitless dancers, with music/live accompaniment. All dancers begin walking or jogging around each other. Be aware of each other and the space around you. Suddenly, upon impulse, one person freezes in a still shape. As you notice this dancer among you, go to him and in response to his shape, connect physically to him and to the other dancers, as do the molecules of a crystal. The full crystal is formed when all the dancers are connected.

▶ The central dancer who began the formation now begins to repeat a movement and sound impulse. When it is felt and heard, the impulse is repeated, first by the dancers closest to the source and eventually by the whole group. In this way the impulse spreads outward through the group, like the rings from a stone thrown into water. As it continues to expand, the impulse will break the physical connections of the group and the dancers will separate from each other, spreading outward into the space. When the energy of the impulse reaches its highest point, this outward expansion stops and the walking and jogging that began the exercise will resume. More than one dancer may initiate a crystal at the same time, in which case the group will divide to join different crystals.

COMPOSITION: IMPROVISATION AND DEVELOPING A THEME

And this was the best of all, and perhaps the greatest of all pedagogical achievements; to be given not only one's artistic independence, but to be forced into an absolute self-responsibility.

(Wigman 1983a: 6)

In the early years at the Wigman School, there was no specific class time set aside to improvise. Instead, improvisation developed as the day's class work progressed. By the time Wigman was teaching in Berlin in the 1950s, the afternoon courses included improvisation, composition and rehearsal time. Students from that time recall the schedule of the afternoon classes: on Mondays and Wednesdays the students would alternate between improvisation and composition taught by Wigman and accompanied by Ulrich Kestler. Tuesdays were for mime class and Thursdays and Fridays were dedicated to dance theory and history. Afternoon rehearsal time was taken up in the development of independent projects that grew out of the composition classes.

IMPROVISATION

Wigman would use imagery to inspire improvisation. She would draw on her own life, whatever was moving her at that time. She also based improvisations on the cardinal elements – fire, water, earth and air – and natural phenomena such as the wind, the quiet snow or falling leaves in the autumn. She also drew on everyday experiences like being on a lonely street. And she used images that had inspired her own dance compositions such as *Schwingende Landschaft* (*Shifting Landscape*, 1929) that traversed a range of emotional experiences in response to an ever-changing natural landscape.

Dance improvisation has become an integral part of the vocabulary of Western modern dance. We have Mary Wigman to thank for this,

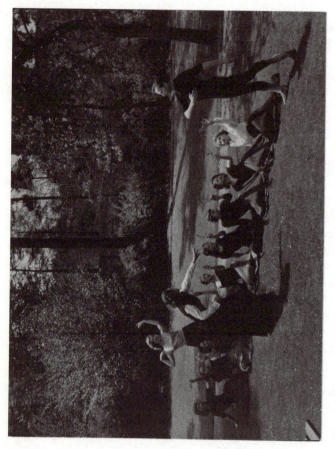

Figure 17 Mary Wigman rehearsing *Carmina Burana* in the garden of the Berlin Wigman School, c. 1955. Photographer unknown, courtesy of the Tanzarchiv Leipzig

in great part. Of course, improvised movement has been a part of dance throughout time and cultures, but the use of improvisation to explore movement ideas for the concert stage has deep roots in Wigman's philosophy of giving the inner experience external shape. Dance improvisation demands a physical way of "being in the moment" that gives substance to the experience of *Dasein* or consciously coming into being in the world. Notably, Wigman didn't encourage the use of improvisation once the dance was crafted and performed onstage. Indeed, her own dances were meticulously shaped into a clear compositional form. But as a tool for movement invention and a means of discovery through physical experience, the addition of improvisation to the language of professional dance continues to permeate the art form and has become a performance technique in itself.

For class, simple improvisations were developed, based on movement themes used by Wigman. In improvisation class the students would sit at Wigman's feet and she would set the improvisation problem or concept for the day. One by one, students would rise and improvise on the spot. A discussion would follow each improvisation and the students would be asked which element they felt was strongest in their work: timing, space, energy/effort or overall design. Try this method of reflection when exploring the following improvisations. The first is designed to be more formal or abstract and the second more dramatic or psychological.

EXERCISES 4.23: STRUCTURED IMPROVISATION

▶ Begin with an assignment based on formal dance elements. You can start simply with an assignment like "Circle into Straight" or "Attraction toward Depth." You can also progress toward more complex images like "Conflict Between the Attractions of Two Opposing Focal Points" or "Building Excitation Leading to Collapse." Let the improvisation arise spontaneously in the moment of showing.

▶ Following the improvisation, allow each dancer to discuss those elements they found strongest in their work as outlined above. The beauty of this sort of spontaneous improvisation is that it reveals which concepts each dancer has grasped deeply and integrated fully into their dance vocabulary.

▶ Next, create an improvisation in response to an emotional situation such as "being on a lonely street" or an action such as "wandering" or an improvisation reflecting a facet of the natural world such as the quiet snow or a sandy beach.

Figure 18 Mary Wigman teaching in her Berlin studio. Photographer unknown, courtesy of the Tanzarchiv Berlin

Look outside your door or window for an improvisational idea. And look within to your own experiences.

▶ The possibilities for either improvisation are limitless.

EXERCISE 4.24: COMPOSITION

▶ We've seen that Wigman had definite ideas about the nature of dance compo-sition. In her composition classes, she often expanded on improvisations by requiring that the students develop a motif or theme. The motivation for the theme in composition class could be a deeper exploration of pure form such as "Circle into Straight" or it might be based on a composition of Wigman's own making. Sometimes she would give a set phrase or a section of one of her choreographed works and ask the students to finish or develop it. The students would work alone or with a partner, and would continue to work on their com-positions outside of the class period. When it was time to show a study, Mary Wigman would ask questions from her chair, such as: "How did you think Sally developed this?" or "How would you [the other students] do it?" This sort of compositional study and critique has become *de rigueur* in choreography classes, particularly in the university setting, but it really emerged in the world of concert dance with the early moderns such as Mary Wigman, Doris Humphrey and Louis Horst.

EXERCISE 4.25: DEVELOPING A THEME

▶ Now, can you extract a movement theme from one or each of your improvisations from exercises 4.23 or 4.24? Recall that Wigman defined the theme as a series of small, related movements. What movements do you recall from your improvisation that relate to each other and could be developed as a phrase to be manipulated and amplified? Consider that Wigman called a theme the base from which the entire composition rests. Craft your theme. Then begin to develop it by keeping in mind those elements of timing, space and energy/effort. Show your theme. Then show how you have chosen to develop it. Let those watching discuss how the theme was developed. Ask others how they would develop the same theme.

ONE FINAL THEME

Mary Wigman wrote that in all of her teaching, "I have attempted to open roads for my pupils leading deep within themselves and to bring them to the point where knowledge and divination become oneness, where experience and creativity penetrate each other." (Wigman 1966: 9) She sought this unity in her own performance and meant to share it through her choreography and teaching as well. Her parting writings expose her desire to "Keep the artistic fire from being extinguished – hold high the torch!" (Wigman 1966: 11) She sought the heroic even as her life unfolded amid tragedy and human failings. Her human nature held blind spots that she never acknowledged publicly. We glimpse them in the private struggles found in her diary entries. Her passion, determination and charisma have become legendary. As have her innovative contributions to the art of dance. She remains controversial to this day. Through grand successes and equally great disappointments, tragedies and misjudgements, she persisted. The story of her life and the themes of her work are epic. And she continued to the end with eyes wide open, even as her vision dimmed.

Teach your students to see and to absorb with waking eyes the manifold eventfulness of their everyday life … teach them to think in terms of big dimensions. The spatial relationships do not tolerate any narrow-minded limitations. They demand a spiritual expansion in the same degree in which the dance gesture strives for faraway space.

(Wigman 1966: 109)

From this perspective it is possible to see Wigman's life as a single great composition. Her story unfolds on that stage where is played out the sweeping drama of human history. Of the larger composition of her own life Wigman wrote:

There has always been only one theme around which my thoughts circled like moths around a light: *Dance* … that is what I want to write about. For you, my friends; for you my students for you who come after me and for all of you who love the dance.

(Wigman 1966: 8–9)

Figure 19 *Abschied und Dank* (Farewell and Thanksgiving) 1942. Photo by Charlotte Rudolf, courtesy of Deutsche Tanzarchiv Köln

SELECTED BIBLIOGRAPHY

BOOKS AND JOURNALS

Anonymous ("L.P.M." probably Louise Martin) (1927) "A Ballet Feud; New Opposition for the Classical School Is Threatened With the Present Invasion Of German Physical Culture," *New York Times*, 25 December, X13.

Bach, Rudolf (1933) *Das Mary Wigman Werk*, Dresden: Carl Reissner.

Bell-Kanner, Karen (1991) *The Life and Times of Ellen von Frankenberg*, Chur, Switzerland; New York: Harwood Academic Publishers.

Benjamin, Walter (1968) *Illuminations: Essays and Reflections*, New York: Harcourt Brace Jovanovich.

Bradley, William S. (1986) *Emil Nolde and German Expressionism: A Prophet in His Own Land*, Ann Arbor: University of Michigan Research Press.

Bronner, Stephen E. and Kellner, Douglas (eds) (1983) *Passion and Rebellion: The Expressionist Heritage*, New York: Columbia University Press.

Buch, David J. and Worthen, Hana (2007) "Ideology in Movement and a Movement in Ideology: The Deutsche Tanzfestspiele 1934 (9–16 December, Berlin)," *Theatre Journal*, 59, 215–39.

Cohen, Marshall and Copeland, Roger (eds) (1983) *What Is Dance? Readings in Theory and Criticism*, New York and Oxford: Oxford University Press.

Cuomo, Glenn (ed.) (1995) *National Socialism and Art*, New York: St. Martin's Press.

De Mille, Agnes (1991) *Martha: The Life and Work of Martha Graham*, New York: Random House.

Dissanayake, Ellen (1988) *What Is Art For?* Seattle and London: University of Washington Press.

Dixon, C. Madeleine (1931) "Mary Wigman," *Theatre Arts Monthly*, 15, 1, 37–42.

Fraleigh, Sondra (1999) *Dancing into Darkness: Butoh, Zen, and Japan*, Pittsburgh: University of Pittsburgh Press.

Fritsch-Vivié, Gabriele (1999) *Mary Wigman*, Reinbek bei Hamburg: Rowohlt Taschenbuch Verlag.

Fulbrook, Mary (1991) *A Concise History of Germany*, Cambridge and New York: Cambridge University Press.

Gitelman, Claudia, compiler and ed. (2003) *Liebe Hanya: Mary Wigman's Letters to Hanya Holm*, Madison: University of Wisconsin Press.

Green, Martin (1986) *Mountain of Truth: The Counterculture Begins Ascona, 1900–1920*, Hanover and London: University Press of New England.

Heidegger, Martin (1935) "The Origin of the Work of Art," in (ed.) D. Krell, *Basic Writings from Being and Time (1927) to The Task of Thinking (1964)*, San Francisco: Harper Collins, 139–212.

—— (1962) *Being and Time*, New York: Harper and Row.

Holm, Hanya (1992) "The Mary Wigman I Knew," in (ed.) W. Sorell, *The Dance Has Many Faces*, Pennington, N.J.: A Capella Books.

Howe, Dianne S. (1987) "The Notion of Mysticism in the Philosophy and Choreography of Mary Wigman, 1914 – 1931," *Dance Research Journal*, 19, 1, 19–24.

—— (1996) *Individuality and Expression: The Aesthetics of the New German Dance, 1908–1936*, New York: P. Lang.

Huelsenbeck, Richard (1969) *Memoirs of a Dada Drummer*, Berkeley: University of California Press.

Huelsenbeck, Richard and Green, Malcolm R. (eds) (1993) *The Dada Almanac*, London: Atlas Press.

Humphrey, Doris (1959) *The Art of Making Dances*, New York: Rinehart Press.

Hurok, Sol, with Goode, Ruth. (1946) *Impresario*, New York: Random House.

Huxley, Michael (1983) "European Early Modern Dance," in (eds) Janet Adshead-Lansdale and June Layson, *Dance History: An Introduction*, London: Dance Books.

Jaques-Dalcroze, Emile (1967) *Rhythm, Music and Education*, trans. Harold F. Rubenstein, London: Dalcroze Society.

Jeschke, Claudia and Vettermann, Gabi (2000) "Germany: Between Institutions and Aesthetics: Choreographing Germanness?" in (eds) Andree Grau, and Stephanie Jordan, *Europe Dancing: perspectives on theatre dance and cultural identity*, London and New York: Routledge.

Johnson, Robert A. (1987) *Ecstasy: Understanding the Psychology of Joy*, New York: HarperCollins.

Jowitt, Deborah (1988) *Time and the Dancing Image*, New York: W. Morrow.

Kant, Marion (2005) Book Review: Mary Wigman and Hanya Holm: A Special Relationship: "Liebe Hanya: Mary Wigman's Letters to Hanya Holm." *Dance Chronicle*, 28, 3, 417–23.

Karina, Lilian and Kant, Marion (2004) *Hitler's Dancers: German Modern Dance and the Third Reich*, New York and Oxford: Berghahn Books.

Koegler, Horst (1974) "In the Shadow of the Swastika: Dance in Germany, 1927–36," *Dance Perspectives*, 57.

Kriegsman, Sali Ann (1981) *Modern Dance in America: The Bennington Years*, Boston, Mass.: G.K. Hall.

Laban, Rudolf von (1975) *A Life for Dance*, trans. Lisa Ullman, New York: Theatre Arts Books.

Lawrence, D.H. (1927) *Mornings in Mexico*, New York: Alfred A. Knopf.

Lehmann-Haupt, Hellmut (1954) *Art Under a Dictatorship*, New York: Oxford University Press.

London, John (ed.) (2000) *Theatre Under the Nazis*, Manchester: Manchester University Press.

McDonagh, Don (1970) *The Rise and Fall and Rise of Modern Dance*, New York: New American Library.

McNeil, William (1995) *Keeping Together in Time: Dance and Drill in Human History*, Cambridge: Harvard University Press.

Maletic, Vera (1987) *Body – Space – Expression: The Development of Rudolf Laban's Movement and Dance Concepts*, Berlin, New York and Amsterdam: Mouton de Gruyter.

Manning, Susan (1993) *Ecstasy and the Demon: Feminism and Nationalism in the Dances of Mary Wigman*, Berkeley: University of California Press.

Martin, John (1929) "Kreutzberg; Brilliant Exponent of German School Transcends It – Current Programs A Misunderstood Movement. Art, Not Propaganda. A School by Himself," *New York Times*, 27 January. X8.

—— (1930) "A Futile Congress; A Low Level of Achievement, With Much Bitter Dissension, Marks Munich Gathering – A Few Fine Performances," *New York Times*, 27 July, X6.

—— (1930) "Mary Wigman's Art; Years of Struggle Have Brought Her to the Very Pinnacle of the German Dance Movement, With a Great Following," *New York Times*, 3 August, 101.

—— (1931) "Dynamic Art; Mary Wigman's Debut Brings an Insight Into German Movement – New Programs A Theatrical Quality. Music and the Dance," *New York Times*, 4 January, X4.

—— (1931) "Cordial Reception For Mary Wigman; A Cycle of Six New Dances Called 'Opfer' Makes Up Most of Her Program. Magnificent Yet Simple Chanin Theatre is Crowded to Its Capacity – A Warm Welcome Accorded the Artist," *New York Times*, 14 December, X17.

—— (1932) "Festival Of Dance Opened By Wigman; Her Group Makes Its American Debut In Cycle Of 8 Numbers Entitled 'Der Weg.' Shadows' Seen As Climax One Of Dances An Effective Piece Of Grotesquerie – Miss Wigman Without A Solo Role," *New York Times*, 26 December, 26.

—— (1933) "Frau Mary Wigman and her Company; The Deadlock Presented by an Individual and a Group – Programs of the Week," *New York Times*, 15 January, X2.

—— (1933) "Gala Farewell by Mary Wigman; Dancer is Recalled a Dozen Times and Finally Has to Make a Speech. to Be Gone Two Years 'Der Feier,' Not Seen Here This Season, Concludes a Performance Unusually Brilliant," *New York Times*, 6 March, 16.

—— (1933a) *The Modern Dance*, Princeton, N.J.: Princeton Book Co.; Dance Horizons, 1989 (Republication of original 1933 edn, New York: A.S. Barnes & Co.).

—— (1936) *America Dancing: The Background and Personalities of the Modern Dance*; photographs by Thomas Bouchard, New York: Dodge Publishing Co.

Martin, John and Maurice Goldberg (1946) "The Dance: Word from Wigman," *New York Times*, 4 August, Sect. 2, 2.

Mosse, George L. (1961) "The Mystical Origins of National Socialism," *Journal of the History of Ideas*, 22, 81–96.

—— (1964) *The Crisis of German Ideology: Intellectual Origins of the Third Reich*, New York: Grosset and Dunlap.

—— (1968) *Nazi Culture: Intellectual, Cultural and Social Life in the Third Reich*, New York: Grosset and Dunlap.

Müller, Hedwig (1983) "At the Start of a New Era," *Ballett International*, 6, 12, 6–13.

—— (1986a) *Mary Wigman: Leben und Werk der grossen Tanzerin*. Berlin: Quadragia Verlag.

—— (1986b) "Mary Wigman and the Third Reich," *Ballett International*, November, 18–23.

—— (1987) "Wigman and National Socialism," *Ballet Review*, 15, 1, 65–73.

Müller, Hedwig and Servos, Norbert (1982) "From Isadora Duncan to Leni Riefenstahl," *Ballett International*, 5, 4, 15–23.

Newhall, Mary Anne Santos (2000) "Dancing in Absolute Eden," M.A. thesis: University of New Mexico, Ann Arbor: UMI (UMI Number 1400402).

—— (2002) "Uniform Bodies: Mass Movement and Modern Totalitarianism," *Dance Research Journal*, 34, 1, Summer: 27–50.

Nietzsche, Friedrich (1966) *Thus Spoke Zarathustra* trans. W. Kaufmann, New York: Viking Press.

Partsch-Bergsohn, Isa (1994) *Modern Dance in Germany and the United States: Crosscurrents and Influences*, Chur, Switzerland: Harwood Academic Publishers.

Partsch-Bergsohn, Isa and Bergsohn, Harold (2003) *The Makers of Modern Dance in Germany: Rudolf Laban, Mary Wigman, Kurt Joos*, Highstown, N.J.: Princeton Book Co.

Preston-Dunlop, Valerie (1988) "Laban and the Nazis" *Dance Theatre Journal*, 6, 2, 4–7.

—— (1998) *Rudolf Laban: An Extraordinary Life*, London: Dance Books.

Preston-Dunlop, Valerie and Lahusen, Susanne (eds) (1990) *Schrifttanz: A View of German Dance in the Weimar Republic*, London: Dance Books, Ltd.

Prevots, Naima (1985) "Zurich Dada and Dance: Formative Ferment," *Dance Research Journal*, 17, 1, 3–8.

Prinzhorn, Hans (1921) *Gedichte Mary Wigman gewidmet* (poems dedicated to Mary Wigman) 15.3.1921, Berlin Archiv

—— (1972) *Artistry of the Mentally Ill: A Contribution to the Psychology and Psychopathology of Configuration*, New York: Springer-Verlag.

Rannow, Angela, and Stabel, Ralf (1994) *Mary Wigman in Leipzig*, Leipzig: Tanzwissenschaft.

Reinhardt, Kurt F. (1962) *Germany: 2000 Years*, New York: Frederick Ungar Publishing.

Richter, Hans (1965) *Dada: Art and Anti-Art*, New York: McGraw-Hill.

Schlee, Alfred (1931) "Expressionism in the Dance," *Modern Music*, 8, 1, 12–16.

Schwaen, Kurt (2006) *Erinnerungen an die Tänzerin Mary Wigman*, Berlin: Kurt Schwaen-Archiv.

Selden, Elizabeth (1930) "Germany's Dance Congress Marks a Renaissance in the Art of Motion," *New York Evening Post*, 31 May.

Soares, Janet (1992) *Louis Horst: Musician in a Dancer's World*, Durham, N.C.: Duke University Press.

Sokel, Walter (1964) *The Writer in Extremis: Expressionism in Twentieth-Century German Literature*, New York: McGraw-Hill, 1964.

Sorell, Walter (1969) *Hanya Holm: The Biography of an Artist*, Middletown, Conn.: Wesleyan University Press.

—— (1986) *Mary Wigman: Ein Vermächtnis*, Wilhelmshaven: Florian Noetzel Verlag.

Spotts, Frederic (2003) *Hitler and the Power of Aesthetics*, Woodstock and New York: The Overlook Press.

Steinweis, Alan E. (1993) *Art, Ideology and Economics in Nazi Germany: The Reich Chambers of Music, Theater and the Visual Arts*, Chapel Hill: University of North Carolina Press.

Tallon, Mary Elizabeth (1984) "Appia's Theatre at Hellerau," *Theatre Journal*, 36, 4, December: 495–504.

Toepfer, Karl (1992) "Speech and Sexual Difference in Mary Wigman's Dance Aesthetic," in (ed.) L. Senelick, *Gender and Performance*, Hanover, N.H.: University Press of New England, 260–78.

—— (1997) *Empire of Ecstasy: Nudity and Movement in German Body Culture, 1910–1935*, Berkeley: University of California Press.

Van der Leeuw, Gerardus (1963) *Sacred and Profane Beauty: The Holy in Art*, Nashville, Tenn., and New York: Abingdon Press.

Vanschaik, Eva (1990) "The Mistrust of Life: Relations in Dance Connections between Butoh, Austruckdanz and Dance Theater in Contemporary Experimental Dance" (interview with G. Van des Leeuw), *Ballett Internationale*, 13, 5: 11.

Von Franz, Marie-Luise (1980) *The Psychological Meaning of Redemption Myths in Fairy Tales*, Toronto: Inner City Books.

Wigman, Mary (1927) "Dance and the Modern Woman," *The Dancing Times*.

—— (1931) "Composition in Pure Movement," *Modern Music*, 8, 2, 20–2.

—— (1935) *Deutsche Tanzkunst*, Dresden: Carl Reissner Verlag.

—— (1963) *Die Sprach des Tanzes*, Stuttgart: Ernst Battenberg Verlag.

—— (1966) *The Language of Dance*, trans. W. Sorell. Middletown, Conn.: Wesleyan University Press.

—— (1973) *The Mary Wigman Book: Her Writings*, (ed. and trans. W. Sorell) Middletown, Conn.: Wesleyan University Press.

—— (1983a) "My Teacher Laban," in (eds) Marshall Cohen and Roger Copeland, *What Is Dance? Readings in Theory and Criticism*, New York and Oxford: Oxford University Press, 302–5.

—— (1983b) "The Philosophy of the Modern Dance," in (eds) Marshall Cohen and Roger Copeland, *What Is Dance? Readings in Theory and Criticism*, New York and Oxford: Oxford University Press, 305–7.

VIDEOTAPES

Hanya: Portrait of a Pioneer (1985) Chico, Calif.: The University Foundation, California State University.

Mary Wigman, 1886–1973: When the Fire Dances Between Two Poles (1991) Pennington, N.J.: Dance Horizons Video.

The Makers of Modern Dance in Germany: Rudolph Laban, Mary Wigman, Kurt Jooss (2004) Highstown, N.J.: Dance Horizons Video.

CD-ROM

Lazarus, H. (2004) "Die Akte Wigman," Hildesheim (Deutsches Tanzarchiv Köln) Georg Olms Verlag.

INDEX